NSKRI

TA-FOR

WORD-FORMATION IN SANSKRIT

[WITH SPECIAL REFERENCE TO TADDHITA-FORMATION]

G. RANGARAJAN

Foreword by
K. KUNJUNNI RAJA

SHARADA

SHARADA PUBLISHING HOUSE
DELHI

First Published 1999

ISBN : 81-85616-55-8

Published by B.L. Bansal for
SHARADA PUBLISHING HOUSE
40, Anand Nagar, Inderlok, Delhi - 110035
Phones: 5117390, 5116763
Typeset by Neographics
1800 Gyani Bazar, Kotlamubarakpur, New Delhi - 110003
and Printed at Santosh Offset,
Delhi - 110035

CONTENTS

FOREWORD

I have great pleasure in writing a Foreword to this interesting doctoral thesis of Dr. G. Rangarajan, Visiting Assistant Professor, Division of Languages, University of South Florida, Tampa, U.S.A. prepared under the guidance of Professor Siniruddha Dash of the Department of Sanskrit, Madras University. It is a study of Word-Formation in Sanskrit with special reference to the *Taddhita*-suffixation; and is modelled on *The Theory of Word-Formation* by M. Aronoff. The author is familiar with the basic works of Chomsky, and Lexicalist Hypothesis of Aronoff, Selkirk and others suggesting that the arguments proposed by Chomsky in his *Remarks* must be extended to all kinds of Derivational Morphology.

The *Taddhita*-Formation belongs to the secondary type of Word-Formation in the *Pāṇinian* tradition. The attempt here is to put the *Taddhita*-Formation pattern in the jacket of Aronoff's Theory of Word-Formation. Aronoff's theory is based mainly on English; and the structure of Sanskrit. Modern Linguistics developed as a result of the discovery of Sanskrit by western scholars; the theories of most of the leaders were influenced by *Pāṇini's*. Mutually conflicting theories which came in the field of linguists in the course of the century have each claimed that it was inspired by *Pāṇini*. Bloomfield who is considered as the father of modern linguistics was a student of Sanskrit; and kept a text of *Pāṇini's sutras* under his pillow; though he wanted to banish semantics from language studies to make linguistics a science. When I worked under Professor J. Brough on 'Indian Theories of Meaning' in SOAS, London, I was advised to submit the thesis to the Sanskrit Department and not to the Linguistics Department, lest the examiners reject it as not coming in the field of linguistics, De Saussure's theory on the basic binary relationship between the word and the meaning was influenced by Indian Theory of *Śabdārtha-Sambandha,* and attacked by the *tringle of meaning* theory of Ogden and Richards. Later Chomsky came with fresh ideas about the importance of syntax and semantics in language studies. His distinction between the surface of meaning and the deep structure of meaning was welcomed by Sanskritists who claimed that the theory had been proclaimed by *Pāṇini* himself in his distinction between the *vibhaktis* and *kārakas.* The Indian studies on *Śābdabodha* was explained as an attempt to convert the surface layer meaning in the unambiguous deep structure level. The present work suggests that Aronoff's theory of word-formation can be interpreted within the *Pāṇinian* system.

The *Pāṇini's* system of *Taddhita* compounds takes into consideration both the form and the meaning involved; but it has to be remembered that *Pāṇini* gave more importance to the correct form than to meaning because he knew that the meaning depends on the usage of the people, and is liable for change and fluctuation. Some of the meanings assigned to special words by *Pāṇini* later became out of date (*āścaryam anitye*); sometimes he gives the meaning in a general way. In case of the desiderative forms, *Pāṇini* gives the suffix in *guptijkidbhyaḥ san,* followed by *'mān -'* and then only the meaning in the next *sūtra dhātōh samānakartṛkād icchāyām* Hence the *sannanta* forms derived by the two previous *sūtras* should not be used in *icchāyām.* The words *jugupsā, cikitsā, mīmāmsā* are correct words, and their meanings are well known in usage.

The *Taddhita* suffixes have been classified into *vācakas* (or *asvārthikas*) and *dyotaka* (or *svārthikas*); This classification is not in *Pāṇini,* but given by his commentators. The sub-classification has been explained by the author. *Pāṇini* has specified nearly 175 meaning headings, each constituting an *Adhikāra.*

Dr. Rangarajan refers to Saroja Bhate's view that *'Pāṇini* has been quite inconsistent with regard to the meaning types that are stated in TF on the ground that the meaning-*adhikāras* which are used in TF are not correlated to the other sections of the *Aṣṭādhyāyī* and that the kaleidoscopic view on the *Taddhita* section in *Aṣṭādhyāyī* is due to multiple authorship', and that TFR-s that fall under the groups where there is a diversity in the meaning *Adhikāras* not formed by *Pāṇini*'. Dr. Rangarajan does not accept this view.

I am glad that modern scholars are trying to check the *Pāṇinian* system on the basis of new theories brought about by modern linguistics, I am equally glad that Pāṇini is still relevant to modern linguistic studies.

K. KUNJUNNI RAJA
Director
The Adyar Library and Research Centre,
Chennai

PREFACE

The present work represents the research work completed under the guidance of Dr. Siniruddha Dash, Prof., Department of Sanskrit, University of Madras. It is a study of Word-Formation in Sanskrit with special reference to the *Taddhita*-suffixation and is modelled upon the work—*The Theory of Word-Formation* by Aronoff.

I take this opportunity to express my thanks and deep sense of gratitude to the authorities of the University for the kind permission accorded to me to pursue my Ph.D Course in the Department of Sanskrit, University of Madras.

To the authorities of the UGC, I am grateful for providing me with the Junior Research Fellowship to carry on my research work.

To my preceptors—Mm Peri Suryanarayana Sastri and Sri U. Ve Srivatsankacarya, I offer my respectful salutations. To them I owe my knowledge of Sanskrit Grammar.

I am thankful to Prof. K. Kunjunni Raja, Director, Adyar Library and Research Centre, Chennai, who willingly agreed to go through the manuscript and write a Foreword to the book.

I will be failing in my duty if I do not record my grateful thanks to Dr. Siniruddha Dash who guided my research work with great sense of participation and commitment.

I express my deep debt of gratitude to Dr. N. Veezhinathan, formerly Professor and Head of the Department of Sanskrit for his valuable suggestions, help and constant encouragement in completing this work.

I have great pleasure in expressing my gratitude to Prof. P. Dasgupta, University of Hyderabad, Prof. Aditi Mukherjee, Osmania University, Prof. Amirthavalli, CIEFL, Prof. Rajendra Singh, University of Montreal, Dr. Joga Singh, Saurashtra

University, Gujarat, for their valuable suggestions and constructive criticisms.

I am thankful to Miss S. Usha and Miss R. Saraswathi for helping me a great deal in the preparation of the work.

To Thiru S. Babu Rajendran of the Department of Sanskrit for the meticulous care and readiness with which he prepared the thesis, I am greatly indebted.

To Thiru K.P. Kunjunni of the Department of Sanskrit, I express my thanks for the courteous service he has rendered throughout my period of study in the Department.

University of Madras, G. RANGARAJAN

ABBREVIATIONS

A	AṢṬĀDHYAYĪ OF PĀṆINI
Mbh.	PATAÑJALI'S MAHĀBHĀṢYA
SK	SIDDHĀNTA KAUMUDĪ

CHAPTER I
INTRODUCTION

1.0. Word-Formation, in general, is the process of derivation of a new word out of an existing one which is technically known as base which may be a word or a root or a stem. The process involves change of a noun into an adjective, of a noun into a verb and the like. This we notice in the case of (1) adjective like *seasonal* which is derived from the noun *season*, and (2) noun *singer* from the verb *sing*, etc. The Word-Formation is, mainly of two types; namely, affixation and compounding. Of these, the former is the addition of an affix to a base which may either be a root or a stem or a word. The latter is the formation of a new word by the addition of two or more free lexemes.

Affixes are further divided into two types: Inflectional and Derivational. Inflectional includes those affixes by adding which we get a form similar to its base, whereas Derivational ones give rise to a new word, the form of which is different from that of its base.[1]

Before descending into details we shall set forth the nature and scope of Word-Formation in general.

1.0.1. *The Nature and Scope of Word-Formation*

Generative grammar in its earlier phase presented a comprehensive theory of grammar with only two main components - syntax and phonology. And morphology has not received the attention it deserves at the hands Generative Transformationalists. The two important works, namely, *Aspects of the Theory of Syntax* by Chomsky for syntax and *The Sound Pattern of English* by Chomsky and Halle for phonology, highlight the theory of Transformational Generative Syntax and Generative Phonology respectively.

To Begin with, in *Aspects*, Chomsky proposed that those formatives which are members of major lexical categories, that is, nouns, verbs, adjectives and adverbs should be regarded as complex symbols made up of various types of features. A large portion of his book is devoted to a discussion on different types of syntactic features. But the last section entitled *The Structure of the Lexicon* is chiefly devoted to a discussion on the morphological phenomena. Several years later Chomsky himself elaborated some of his earlier theories. In his paper *Remarks on Nominalization* he gave a fresh impetus to the role of morphology in Generative Grammar and thereby explicitly claimed that the derivation of certain complex words must be treated outside the scope of syntactic rules. This claim though couched in modern formal terms is in effect a return to the traditional view according to which Derivational Morphology or Word-Formation is distinct from syntax.

1.0.2. Transformational Generative Grammar in its nascent stage was axiomatic in character. Two sentences which convey an identical sense differ from each other in so far as their structure is concerned. The order of words found in one sentence would be changed in the transformed sentence and, in the same way, certain words found in the one would be deleted in the other while certain words not found in the one would be added in the other. Further the transformed sentence would consist of new morphemes arranged or placed in a fixed order. For example:

> The cat swallows the milk.
> The milk is swallowed by the cat.

Here the logical significance of the two sentences is the same. Yet there is change in their structure. The processes through which changes in the structure occur may be explained by what is known as Transformational Rules [TR] in a manner so as to be applicable to all cases of the above kind. The rule is:

NP_1	V	+	Tense	NP_2	- 4BE	EN	+	3 +	2	+ By + 1
.	2		3	4						

This one identifies the changes in the order of the words in the two sentences. Further it implies the absolute necessity of the insertion of certain morphemes such as *ed* or *been* and *by*.

Influenced by the above rule, Lees [1960] argued[2] that within the framework of transformational rules of the above kind, one could derive complex nominal words too. According to him, for deriving a complex nominal word, there must be a sentence serving as its underlying principle. For example:

Robin is devoted to her mother.
Robin's devotion to her mother.

Herein the complex nominal word - Robin's Devotion is derived by the application of a different kind of transformation rule from the first sentence which naturally serves as the base or ground.

Chomsky, however, does not favour the above view. He argues that the application of the transformational rule wherein Syntactic transformation is inherent cannot be extended to the derivation of complex nominal words. It is because the meanings of the complex nominal words *destruction, marriage* and *trial* derived from words like *destroy, marry* and *try* differ from those of latter. But the two forms - one of which is derived from the other by the application of the TR - do not differ from each other in so far as their meaning-content is concerned. Hence in the cases cited above the meanings of the complex nominal words differ from the verbs out of which they are derived. It is precisely on this ground Chomsky has rejected the extention of the TR to the derivation of complex nominal words.

A careful study of Chomsky's *Remarks* goes to prove that the complex nominal words could not be derived by the application of the TR. He selects certain verbal forms from each one of which two different kinds of complex nominal words are derived. For example :

Base	***Complex***	***Nominal Word***
approve	approval	approbation

commit	committal	commitment
employ	employ	employment
join	junction	juncture

In the above cases the meanings of the complex nominal words differ from those of their bases and also between themselves. This has led Chomsky to arrive at the conclusion that the application of the TR does not bring in the identity of the meanings of the bases and the output.

It must be noted here that the resultant forms arrived at by the application of the TR have definitely their respective bases, and, the meaning of the base and that of the resultant form by the application of the TR remain to be the same. In the case of complex nominal words, however, we notice that the derived words such as *exigency, notion*, etc., do not have any verb as their base. Further there are some verbs which have no complex nominal words at all. For example: *come, eat, open, see*, etc.

From the above discussion it follows that according to Chomsky nominalisation could not be arrived at by the application of the Syntactic Transformation Rules.

On the basis of the evidences adduced by Chomsky in his *Remarks on Nominalization*, Morris Halle in his *Prolegomena to a Theory of Word-Formation*, Jackendoff in his *Morphological and Semantic Regularities in the Lexicon*, Aronoff in his *Word-Formation in Generative Grammar* and Selkirk in her *Syntax of Words*, proposed an autonomous morphological component within the framework of Chomsky's views, widely known as Lexicalist Hypothesis. The primary motive of this school is that Derivational Morphology must be dealt with within the lexicon. On this ground this school is referred to as the school of Lexicalist Morphology.[3] The objective of this school is that the arguments proposed by Chomsky in his *Remarks* must be extended to all kinds of Derivational Morphology. It must be noted here that Chomsky did not propose a theory of morphology; rather he merely suggested that the Derivational Morphology must be isolated from syntax thus precluding the possibility of syntax covering Derivational Morphology.

1.0.3. In the above light, Aronoff established the theory of Word-Formation which separates Derivational Morphology from that of Syntax. Aronoff states the objective of morphology thus:

"Just as the simplest goal of a syntax is the enumeration of the class of possible sentences of a language so the simplest task of a morphology, the least we demand of it, is the enumeration of the class of possible words of a language"; Or, in rather different terms, "It is the task of a morphology to tell us what sort of new words a speaker can form".[4]

In a Grammar which builds up stems and words from an already existing item there is a set of regular and interesting rules which Aronoff characterizes as Word-Formation Rules (WFR) which we shall discuss now.

Features of Word-Formation Rules

Word Formation Rules (WFR) have four types of Linguistic Features which are as follows:

(1) Range of Application;
(2) Pronunciation, Stress/Accent, etc; (Phonological and the Supra-segmental properties of the base as well as the output);
(3) Syntactic category; and,
(4) Meaning change.

1. *Range of Application*

WFR identify the base of the new words as either a word or a stem or a root.

2. *Pronunciation, Stress/Accent, etc.*

The Pronunciation of the derived word is specified in a WFR. Oftentimes the pronunciation of the new word is merely the combination of the pronunciation of its parts; but in certain cases there is change in the pronunciation of the derived word in a regular manner. Similarly in so far as the Stress/Accent is concerned, the words generally differ from their own base. It comes to this: the derived word will attain a different stress pattern and the accent of the same will also change depending upon the context.

3. *Syntactic Category*

A WFR specifies the syntactic category of the base as well as the output. And, by its application the category of the base is also changed. For example, according to Aronoff, the base out of which a new word is to be derived must be a member of a major syntactic category. That is, the base must be either a noun or a verb; or, it must be an adjective or an adverb.[5]

4. *Meaning Change*

Each Affix has more or less a significant impact upon the meaning of the stem. When we analyse the process of WFR we could notice the difference in the meaning of the output from that of the base.

In regard to Word-Formation in general, Aronoff has distinct views out of which five are important to our study of the *Taddhita*-Formation [*TF*] in the present work. We shall now set forth those views in detail.

First View

Aronoff holds the view that Derivational Morphology should not be treated as part of Transformational Generative Grammar wherein TRs are embedded; on the other hand, he states that it should be given an independent status.

When advocating this view Aronoff has been greatly influenced by the view of Chomsky according to which TR cannot be applied to the derivation of complex nominal words on the ground that the latter are semantically irregular.[6] And, so there is the need for a separate theory to deal with the problems connected with the derivation of complex nominal words. Such a separate theory is termed the theory of Word-Formation.

Second View

In regard to the range of application of the WFR Aronoff states as follows:

i. all regular Word-Formation processes are Word-based;
ii. a new word is formed by applying a regular rule to a single already existing word; and,
iii. both the new word and the existing one are members of major lexical categories.[7]

These three constitute what is known as Word-Based Hypothesis (WBH).

Aronoff's observation implies the following:

1. the bases of WFR's must be words; and they must be existing ones. A possible but non-existent word cannot serve as the base of a WFR;
2. WFR's can take neither a phrase nor a bound form but only a single word; and,
3. the input as well as the output of a WFR must be members of a major lexical category.

Third View

WBH mentioned in the previous paragraph should be applicable to the Word-Formation in all the languages.

Fourth View

Unitary Base Hypothesis (UBH)

The relation between a suffix and a base is unalterably fixed. That is, a suffix can be applied to either a noun or a verb and not to both.[8]

Fifth View

A Grammar of any language consists of four major linguistic features, namely, (1) Phonological, (2) Morphological, (3) Syntactic, and (4) Semantic. And any WFR must involve reference to these features.[9]

Of these five views, it is only the last view with which we are chiefly concerned, as the *Taddhita*-Formation Rules [TFR] are discussed in the following pages in relation to the Phonological, Morphological, Syntactic and Semantic features.

To sum up this part of the discussion

Derivational Morphology which was considered to be a part of Transformational Generative Syntax for a long period of time has been proved in recent times to be a distinct branch of study, as the rules of the latter are not efficacious to explain fully the theories involved in the former.

In this connection Chomsky has observed that "much of derivational morphology is semantically irregular and should not be handled in the syntax".[10] His observation has paved the way for viewing Derivational Morphology as a branch different from Transformational Generative Syntax. Following Chomsky's observation, M. Halle, Jackendoff, Aronoff and others have upheld the independent status for Derivational Morphology.

Among the above linguists, Aronoff further developed the theory of Derivational Morphology known as Word-Formation by putting forward various proposals such as Word-Based Hypothesis, Unitary Base Hypothesis, etc. The present work is based upon the views of Aronoff.

We shall now deal with the scope of Word-Formation in Sanskrit.

1.1.0. Unlike in Modern Linguistics, there is no explicit reference to the distinction between Syntax and Morphology in Pāṇini's *Aṣṭādhyāyī*. But an analysis of the various methods adopted by Pāṇini to explain the syntactic and semantic relation that underlie the *Kāraka*-relations enables one to assume that such a distinction is implicit in the *Aṣṭādhyāyī*. As observed by Singh J.D [1975:297] "the representation of *Kāraka*-relations by inflectional endings on the one hand and by derivative suffixes and nominal compound constructions on the other differs significantly. In the case of the former the output is a syntactic construction while in the latter it is a morphological one".[11]

1.1.1 The notion of *Kāraka* plays a vital role in the linguistic theory of Pāṇini. The *Kāraka*-relations essentially serve to connect words - nouns and verbs through their meanings. And the relation of the meaning is known as syntactic meaning. In other words, the *Kāraka*-theory of Pāṇini deals with the noun-verb relation in a sentence. At the syntactic level, these relations are denoted by inflectional suffixes added to their bases. For example, *devadattaḥ odanam pacati* - 'Devadatta cooks rice'. Here the verbal ending - *ti* denotes *kartā* while the nominal ending - *am* that is added to the stem *odana* signifies *karma*. Similarly in *devadattena pakvaḥ odanaḥ* - 'the rice was cooked by Devadatta', the primary derivative suffix - *kta* added to the verb *pac* - 'to cook' expresses *karma*, while the nominal ending - *ktā* added to the stem devadatta expresses *kartā*.[12]

1.1.2. The *Kāraka*-Relations are denoted by complex morphological forms too. At the morphological level, that is, in derived nominal stems, the *Kāraka*-relations are expressed by primary (*kṛt*) or secondary (*taddhita*) suffixes and by compound words. For example, in *śrotṛ*- 'a listener' the primary suffix-*tṛC* added to the verbal root *śru*- 'to listen' expresses *kartā* (A. 3.4.67). In analytical syntactic construction, namely, *śruṇoti yaḥ* the - *ti* expresses the *kartā*. Similarly the word *vaiyā-karanaḥ* is derived by the addition of the suffix - *a Ṇ* to the Nominal word *vyākaraṇa (am)*. The underlying syntactic structure of the word *vaiyakaranaḥ* is *vyākaraṇam adhīte*. Here the verbal suffix-*te* expresses the *kartā*-relation and the nominal case-ending - *am* signifies the *karma*-relation. In compound words such as *māsadeyam (ṛṇam)* - 'a (debt) to be paid off in a month', the underlying syntactic structure is *mase deyam*. Here the first constituent member, namely, *mase* denotes the *adhikaraṇa*-relation.

From the above it is evident that the *Kāraka*-relationship is signified through the Inflectional suffixes on the one hand and the Derivational type of suffixes or compound words on the other. The former one comes under the purview of Inflectional Morphology, while the latter under Derivational Morphology.

The above two major devices adopted by Pāṇini to represent the *Kāraka*-relations show that he favours the distinction between Syntax and Morphology.

1.1.3. The conclusion arrived at in the previous paragraph may be re-inforced by stating that of the two devices, the inflectional type of suffixation comes under the range of *vibhaktividhi*;[13] and, the derivational type of suffixation and compounding belong to the theory of *padavidhi* (Word-Formation). Pāṇini must have felt that there is no uniform principle to identify the *Kāraka*-relations in general as he adopts two modes to represent the *Kāraka*-relation, namely, *vibhaktividhi* and *padavidhi* applied respectively at the syntactic and the morphological level. This leads us to conclude that the distinction between Syntax and Morphology is inherent in the grammatical tradition of Pāṇini.

We shall now discuss the *padavidhi* in detail.

1.2.0. The *padavidhi* accounts for the syntactic relations which are found in the underlying syntactic structure. But it alone is not its aim. A detailed analysis of the theory of Word-Formation shows that the theory of *padavidhi* is not restricted to the representation of syntactic relations alone. It explains the many facets of grammar too. It other words, the theory of *padavidhi* not only accounts for the syntactic relations, but also explains the phonological, morphological, syntactic and semantic features of a derived word. It will be relevant to point out here that while explaining the *ekārthī-bhāvasāmarthya*, Patañjali himself distinguishes between the underlying syntactic structures (*vigraha-vākya*) and their corresponding derived words (*vṛtti*). After discussing elaborately the concept of *ekārthībhāvasāmarthya*, Patañjali gives a *resume* of the special features of *ekārthībhāva*. They are:

1. absence of inflectional suffixes after the compound members;
2. non-separation of the constituent members by another word;
3. fixed order of the constituents; and
4. a single accent.[14]

He argues that though the semantics of the underlying syntactic structures and their corresponding derived words are similar, yet there are many features which cannot be attained at the syntactic level. This argument leads us to believe that the distinction between the syntax and morphology is sanctioned by tradition.

1.2.1. The lexicalist hypothesis proposes the separation of the derivational morphology from the transformational generative syntax on the ground that the spheres of their functions are clearly set forth. This is the view of Halle too when he points out that "the character of these rules and their relationship to other parts of the grammar, in particular, to the rules of syntax and of the phonology, has been studied only to a very limited extent".[15] Viewed in the above light, in Sanskrit too the synthesised process of Word-Formation is efficacious to explain only syntactic relations, and not the phonological, morphological and semantic aspects of the grammar. This is probably the reason for Pāṇini treating of the *padavidhi* separately from the other *vidhi*-s such as *vibhaktividhi, aṅgavidhi, varṇavidhi,* etc.

In the following section we shall discuss the different types of Sanskrit Word-Formation.

1.3. *Types of Word-Formation*

A study of the *Aṣṭadhyāyi* shows that in the Sanskrit grammatical tradition there are two types of Word-Formation, namely, (1)Suffixation and (2)Compounding. Of these, suffixation is the addition of a suffix to a base which may either be a verbal root (*dhātu*) or a nominal stem (*prātipadika*) or a word *(pada)*. Suffixes are classified into two: (1) Inflectional; and (2) Derivational. The inflectional type of suffixes includes the nominal endings - *suP* and the verbal endings - *tiṄ*, whereas derivational suffixes encompass *kṛt* (primary derivatives), *taddhita* (secondary derivatives) and the suffixes like - *saN* (desideratives)[16] etc.

1.3.1. *Inflectional Suffixes (Vibhaktividhi)*

When these are added to a stem or a root, the resultant form will be a word. For example:

i. [(rāma) stem + (- sU) suf] word - *ramaḥ* word (N)

ii. [(bhū) root + (- ti) suf] word - *bhavati* word (V)

1.3.2. *Derivational suffixes* on the other hand, comprise of four types which are as follows:

1. Desiderative and causative suffixes (*sanādi*) added to a verbal root;
2. *Kṛt* (primary) suffixes added to a verbal root;
3. Denominal suffixes (*sanādi*) added to a nominal word (*pada*); and,
4. *Taddhita* (secondary) suffixes added to a nominal word.

These may be illustrated as follows:

Base	***Suffix***	***Resultant form***
1. Desiderative and causative suffixes.	[(kṛÑ) + (- saN) - root (suf)] - root	- *cikirṣā* (root)
2. *Kṛt* (primary)	[(kṛÑ) + (- tṛ)] root suf - stem	- *kartṛ* (stem)
3. Denominal suffix (*sanādi*)	[(putram) + (kyaC) word suf] - - root	- putrīya (root)
4. *taddhita* (secondary)	[(dasaratha + Ṅas) + (- iÑ)suf] stem word	- *dāśarathi* (stem)

1.3.3. In the case of compounding the formation of a new word is effected by the addition of two or more free forms. Moreover, the compounding takes place only in the case of words which are related both syntactically and semantically. For example, *rājapuruṣaḥ*. Herein, the word *puruṣa* conveys the sense of a person having relation to the king. The sense of the person is predominant and the sense of relation to the king is subordinate and hence adjectival to it. The word *rāja* merely serves as a factor to indicate the sense in which the *puruṣa* is to be taken. In short, the derived word *rājapuruṣaḥ* denotes a single integrated meaning (*aikārthya*), namely, 'a king's man'.

1.3.4. Differences between Inflectional and Derivational suffixes.[17]

Inflectional	*Derivational*
1. The output is a word (*pada*) that does not admit of any other suffix.	1. The output is either a stem (*prātipadika*) or a root (*dhātu*).
2. No change in the category of the base.	2. There is change in the category of the base.
3. Forms so derived have no alternation with its base.	3. Except *kṛt* formation, the forms that are derived by the addition of these suffixes are optional. As an alternative the underlying sentence may be used.
4. Meanings are fixed	4. Meanings are diverse.

1.4. *Padavidhi and Word-Formation: Their mutual Relation*

While recording the views in regard to the addition of suffixes, we said that (See 1.3) a suffix is added either to a root or to a word (*pada*).[18] In the Pāṇinian tradition a *pada* is defined as that which has a nominal suffix or a verbal one at its end.[19] Now we have to enquire as to whether we shall take the term *pada* involved in the expression - *padavidhi* (A. 2.1.1) in the above sense. This enquiry is necessitated by the fact that the adoption of the term - *pada* in the above sense presents a difficulty in two cases, although no difficulty is noticed in other cases, namely, compounding, addition of *taddhita-*, and the denominal-suffixes and also of the *Upapada-kṛt-* suffixes.[20] It is because in these cases, it is with reference to a *pada* another word, or the *taddhita*, or the denominal, or the *upapada-kṛt-*suffix is added. But the desiderative suffix or the unqualified *kṛt*-suffix[21] is added only to a verbal root and not to a *pada* that has at its and a nominal suffix or the verbal suffix. Thus the application of the definition of *pada* in the case of the term *pada* in the expression *padavidhi* would preclude the possibility of the addition of the desiderative and the un-qualified *kṛt*-suffix, as the base to which they are added is not *pada* in the technical sense of the term. Hence we must take the term *pada* in the expression *padavidhi* not in its technical sense but in the popular sense of that which is significative of a meaning.[22] In other words, the word *pada* in the expression *padavidhi* stands for a free but minimal meaningful unit.

When viewed in the above light, it is easier to account for the formation of the derived words by the addition of the desiderative and the un-qualified *kṛt*-suffix too. The root *kṛñ* to which both the suffixes are added is a minimal meaningful unit. The addition of other suffixes also to the base holds good, as those bases too are meaningful free forms.

It may be added here that the commentators like Patañjali[23] Kaiyaṭa,[24] Jinendrabuddhi and Haradatta[25] take the term *pada* in the expression *padavidhi* in its technical sense and thus hold the view that the base for the addition of the suffixes must be a *pada* in its complete form. This, of course, presents difficulty in the case of the addition of desiderative and un-qualified *kṛt*-suffixes to the base, as the base is not a *pada* in the strict technical sense of the term. Nāgeśa has felt this difficulty[26] and has sought to obviate it by taking the term *pada* in the expression *padavidhi* in the sense of a minimal meaningful unit.

Nāgeśa further argues[27] that the term *pada* in the expression *padavidhi* is specifically used by Pāṇini with a view to emphasize that in the case of application of the morpho-phonological rule leading to a grammatical operation in respect of a letter or *varṇa* the latter need not have *sāmarthya* or the power to convey the unified sense. This would become clear when we consider the sentence:

tiṣṭatu dadhyaśāna tvam śākena

wherein between the letter *i* in *dadhi* and *a* in *aśāna* there is the morpho-phonological operation resulting in the change of *i* to *y*. Here the prescription of the morpho-phonological rule does not depend upon any power or *sāmarthya* on the part of the letter *i*. It comes to this that in order to exclude these cases, Pāṇini has specifically stated that the application of grammatical rule relating to a *pada* would require *sāmarthya* on the part of the latter. And, Pāṇini must have used the term *pada* in the sense of a minimal meaningful unit.[28]

The foregoing explanation allows room for holding that the rules for addition of all suffixes would be applicable, without any exception whatsoever, to all the five varieties of word-formation referred to above.

Nāgeśa's interpretation that the term *pada* in the expression *padavidhi* must be taken in the sense of a minimal meaningful unit is not an arbitrary one. It is permitted or sanctioned by Pāṇini himself. A study of the aphorisms prescribing the rules for suffixation and compounding would show that Pāṇini has never meant a word-form complete in all respects as the significance of the term *pada* in the expression *padavidhi* and as the one that would invariably serve as the base in all cases of suffixation and compounding. If he had meant so, then he need not have stressed the specification of a particular kind of base in respect of compounding, and the addition of the *taddhita*-, and the denominal suffix, and a different kind of base in respect of the addition of the desiderative and the *kṛt* suffix. It is well-known that in regard to the former group, the base is a *pada* in the technical sense of the term and in regard to the latter group it is a verbal-root and not a *pada* in the technical sense of the term. But both the cases would be covered if the word *pada* in the expression *padavidhi* is taken in the sense of a minimal meaningful unit. And, both the word in its complete form and the *verbal-root* are meaningful units.

1.5. The problem as to what could constitute the base for the application of word-formation rules has been engaging the attention of the modern linguists. While Aronoff holds[29] the view that a word serves as the base, Halle is of the view[30] that a minimal meaningful unit or a morpheme could serve as the base. In other words, these two noted linguists advocate what in Modern Linguistic terms are known as *word-based hypothesis* (WBH) and *Morpheme-based hypothesis* (MBH) respectively. Scalise has felt[31] the difficulty which we have identified earlier in the word-based hypothesis and so she prefers the Morpheme-based hypothesis which is otherwise known as *Revised Word-Based Hypothesis.* Thus we see that the views of the traditional grammarians and modern Linguists are identical in this respect.

1.6. *Scope*

The present work is exclusively related to the discussion of the *taddhita* suffixes (TS). The latter may be defined as suffixes which are different from *suP, tiṄ, kṛt* and *sanādi.*[32] The addition of these suffixes to their respective bases brings in certain linguistic changes which are phonological, morphological, syntactic and semantic in character. These features reflected in TF are discussed in detail in the following chapters.

1.6.1. *Methods*

The present work is an attempt to analyse the *Taddhita*-Formation in the light of the Modern Linguistics theory especially the theory of Word-Formation.

1.6.2. *Sources*

The Present Data have been collected from both the primary and the secondary source. The important lexicons of Sanskrit and the grammatical works on Pāṇinian tradition play a major role in providing us with maximum data for this work. The modern research works available on Word-Formation constitute the secondary source.

We shall now discuss the classification of TS in detail.

1.7. *Morphological and Semantic Classification of Taddhita Suffixes*

The *taddhita* suffixes are classified according to the morphological and semantic criteria into two domains, that is, *pratyayādhikāra* and *arthādhikāra*. We shall begin with a discussion on *pratyayādhikāra*.

1.7.1. *Morphological classification of Taddhita Suffixes*

One and the same suffix (say) *-aṆ* set forth in the aphorism - *prāgdīvyato'Ṇ* (*A*.4.1.85) is intended to be applicable to any stem; and, it has the significative power to convey a variety of meanings. The scope of this aphorism extends upto the end of the Third Section of the Fourth Chapter of the *Aṣṭādhyāyī* (*A*.4.3.168). For example, the aphorism *tasyāpatyam* whose range of application extends upto *A*.4.1.178 simply records the sense, namely, an offspring; it does not prescribe any specific suffix apart from *-aṆ*. In such cases, the suffix *-aṆ* is to be applied to the stem to arrive at the sense of 'an offspring'. In this sense the prescription of the suffix *-aṆ* has the restrictive force over a variety of meanings. It is, therefore, designated as *pratyayādhikāra*.

The word derived by the addition of the suffix *aṆ* to the stem *upagu* is *aupagava-* 'a descendent of *upagu*'. This word remains to be the same, while its meanings may differ in accordance with the usages in common experience. In other words, the surface level form of the word will be the same, while its meanings when viewed under different contexts differ. That is, in so far as the deeper level of the word is concerned there is a difference; and in so far as the surface level of the word is concerned there is identity. The details of this classification are given in the Third Chapter of the present work.

1.7.2. *Arthādhikāra* is based on the different meaning headings that cover a variety of suffixes. In other words, the one and the same meaning may be expressed by a number of suffixes. For example, the *apatyadhikāra*. This consists of nearly twenty five suffixes for denoting the single sense of 'an offspring'. Hence, this *adhikāra* is known as *arthādhikāra*. It is identified on the basis of the general meaning-statements found in this section. Thus each meaning-bearing statement has wide range of application covering a variety of suffixes. In other words, a meaning-bearing statement is an *adhikāra*. For example, *tasyāpatyam* (A.4.1.92) *tena raktam rāgāt* (A.4.2.1), *tasya samuhaḥ* (A.4.2.37), *tadadhīte tadveda* (A.4.2.59), etc. These *adhikāra*-s contain reference to manifold suffixes fit to be applied to given bases.

1.7.3. *Semantic Classification of Taddhita Suffixes*

The *Taddhita-Suffixes* may be significant or non-significant. That is, they are either *vācaka*-s or *a-svārthika*-s, or *dyotaka-s* or *svārthika*-s. Of these *a-svārthika* suffixes are those which convey a sense different from the sense of the stem to which they are added. For example, the suffix-*iÑ*. When this suffix is added to the word *daśaratha (sya)*, it conveys the meaning of the son of *daśaratha* which is different from the meaning of the stem *daśaratha*. Hence these are termed as *asvārthika*-suffixes. The suffix-*taL* when applied to the base -*deva* results in the formation of the word *devatā*. Herein, the suffix does not carry any sense different from the meaning of the base. It is, therefore, called a *svārthika*-suffix. The details of this classification are given in the Fifth Chapter of the present work.

Summary

We have so far discussed the nature and the scope of Word-Formation in general and in Sanskrit in particular. Accordingly we have analysed the view of Chomsky which separates the theory of Word-Formation from that of transformational Generative Syntax. Based upon Chomsky's view, Aronoff made an elaborate study on the theory of Word-Formation providing different hypothesis such as WBH, UBH, etc.

Sanskrit WF comes under the domain of *padavidhi*. In this connection we have noticed the importance of *padavidhi* and its various types on the basis of different kinds of bases from which the new words are derived. Further a note is given in regard to the base of Sanskrit WF, (which may either be a word or a stem or a root) to the effect that the *Word-based theory* which is discussed in the Pāṇinian tradition as well as in Modern Linguistics could not be applied in certain cases such as unqualified-*kṛt* formation, desiderative and causative formations. It is because in these cases a verbal-root serves as a base for the *kṛt* and *sanādi* suffixes and not a word. Besides, we have also classified the *Taddhita*-suffixes on the basis of morphological the and semantic characteristics. The former one belongs to the *pratyayādhikāra*, and the latter one to the *arthādhikāra*. Similarly TS are also classified as *asvārthika* and *svārthika*-s.

In the following chapter we shall deal with the Phonological features that are involved in *Taddhita*-Formation.

REFERENCES

1. For details see Section 1.3. of this present work.
2. *The Grammar of English Nominalizations.*
3. Bauer, L., *Introducing Linguistic Morphology*, p. 125.
4. *Word-Formation in Generative Grammar*, pp. 17-19.
5 *Ibid.*
6. We have stated earlier that the sentences derived by the application of *TR* must be semantically regular.
7. *Word-Formation in Generative Grammar*, p. 21.
8. Vide: "The Semantics Syntactic specification of the base though it may be more or less complex is always unique. A WFR will never operate on either this or that". *Ibid*, p. 47.
9. Vide: "There are different kinds of information in a grammar; syntactic, semantic, phonological and morphological. Words, contain information of all these types, and WFRs, as rules for making up new words, most likely introduce all of these types of information as well". *Ibid.*
10. *Remarks on Nominalization.*
11. *Pāṇini's Theory of Kāraka*-s.
12. Representation of Kāraka-relations by inflectional case-endings is described under *A*.2.3.1. which enunciates that *Kāraka*-

relations in a construction are expressed by case-endings in case these are not already represented by any other linguistic element (*anukte karmaṇi dvitiyāsyāt abhihite tu karmaṇi prātipadikārthamatre'ti prathamaiva/abhidhānam ca prāyeṇa tiṄ-kṛttaddhita-samāsaiḥ, SK* on *A*.2.3.1). See also Sec. 3.1 in the present work.

13. This stands for both the declensional suffixes and the verbal suffixes (*suPtiṄau vibhaktisamjñau stah, SK.* on *A*.1.4.104).
14. *subalopovyavadhānam yatheṣṭamanyatareṇābhisambandha-svaraḥ, MBh., Samarthāhnika, Bh.* No. 48.
    See also Introduction on *Bahuvrīhidvandvāhnika.*
15. *Prolegomena to a Theory of Word-Formation*, p. 3.
16. Some of the *sanādi* suffixes are added to the nominal words which some, to the roots.
17. For details see Bauer, L:
    i. *English Word-Formation*, pp. 22-29.
    ii. *Introducing Linguistic Morphology*, pp.12-13.
    See also Scalise: *Generative Morphology*, pp. 102-114.
18. See Sec. 1.3 of the present work.
19. *suPtiṄantam padam, A*.1.4.14.
20. For example, the word *kumbhakāra.* Here the verbal root *kṛñ* is qualified by the word *kumbham* and the grammatical rule is such that the *kṛt* suffix -*aṆ* could be added to *kṛñ* only when it is qualified by an object-word like *kumbham.* This is known as *upapada-kṛt.*
21. This is to exclude the *upapada-kṛt*-suffix mentioned above.
22. *śaktam padam.*
23. vide: *MBh.* on *A*.3.1.92.
24. vide: *Ibid. A*.2.1.1.
25. vide: *Kāśika, A*.2.1.1.
26. *Mañjūṣā (Vṛttivicāra* section),
27. *Ibid.*
28. *tenārthavatsamudāyoddeśyako vidhiḥ samarthāśritaḥ iti sūtrārthaḥ. Ibid.*
29. *Word-Formation in Generative Grammar*, p. 21.
30. *Prolegomena to a Theory of Word-Formation*, p. 10.
31. *Generative Morphology*, pp. 72-75; and also See Bauer, L., *English Word-Formation*, pp. 174-76.

CHAPTER - II

PHONOLOGICAL FEATURES INVOLVED IN TADDHITA-FORMATION

2.0. ***Salient Features of Phonology in Word-Formation***

Generally a Word-Formation Rule specifies a base and also some operations on the base which results in the formation of a new word. This operation will usually have some phonological reflex when we add some morphemes to the base.[1]

A WFR also specifies the phonological form of the affix and its place in relation to the base. For example, in English the suffix - # *ness* is added at the end of a base. Similarly a WFR specifies the boundary which, in the present case, is a word associated with the base. In the above instance, that is, the suffix-*ness* is added to a word.

Apart from these, the phonological operation gives the appropriate pronunciation of the new word in the form of phonetic representation. For example, the affix + *al (+∂l)* is added to the noun-doctrine *('d) ktrin)* which results in a new word-do'ctrinal (d) k'trin∂l). In this way, the pronunciation of the new word is obtained from the phonetic representation. This includes the supra-segmental features such as stress, accent and its tonal properties of the new word.

2.1.0. *Phonological Classification of English Derivational Affixes*

It has long been recognised that English derivational affixes fall into distinct classes with respect to their phonological properties. For example, Chomsky and Halle have taken account of this in their book - *Sound Pattern in English* which treats of the English-Word Phonology, consisting of *non-neutral* and *neutral* affixes. These two are referred to in the above work as Class I affixes which are stress-affecting and

Class II which are stress-neutral respectively. Siegel provides[2] the important insight into the fact that the affix-classes motivated on the basis of phonology also play a crucial role in the description of English derivational morphology, especially in the description of the distribution of affixes within English words. Further the difference between non-neutral and neutral affixes in terms of the boundary elements associated with the affixes is explained in the above work. For example, neutral affixes are preceded or followed by the word-boundary (#) while non-neutral affixes by the morpheme-boundary (+); and, this difference in boundary is claimed to be responsible for the differential behaviour of both the stress rules and the rules of segmental phonology with respect to the affixes. Siegel and Allen who accept this theory of boundary distinction and its role in regard to the rules of segmental phonology and stress rules develop it further.[3]

TO SUM UP: the derivational affixes in English are classified by Chomsky and Halle as Class I affixes and Class II affixes.[4] Of these, the Class I affixes are separated from their stems by a '+' boundary, whereas Class II affixes, by the '#' boundary. This has led the modern linguists to recognise two classes of English affixes: Class I, the stress-affecting affixes, and Class II, the stress-neutral affixes. According to Siegel the Class I affixes are added to both the words as well as stems (morphemes), whereas Class II are added only to words.[5] Allen also seems to favour this view.[6]

2.1.1 There are some English derivational affixes which do affect the stress of the base. They do this either by attracting stress onto themselves or by attracting stress onto a specific syllable that is defined in relation to the suffix. Thus in the following examples[7] the Class I suffixes *+ese* and *+ic* affect the stress of the base:

(a)	journal	journa'lese
	Japan	Japanese
	Official	Officia'lese
(b)	'acid	a'cidic

'poet po'etic
'telescope tele'scopic

On the other hand, Class II affixes like all English inflectional affixes, do not affect the stress of the base.[8] For example, when the suffix # less is added to a base, the stress on the new word remains on the same syllable in the base. This may be illustrated as follows:

'humour 'humourless
'meaning 'meaningless
'character 'characterless
'de'fence 'defenceless
'ex'pression 'ex'pressionless

This approach to word-formation widely known as the Level-Ordered model of affixation that has been incorporated into the revised version of generative phonology is also broadly known as *Lexical Phonology*.[9]

2.1.2. *A Brief Note on Boundaries in Sanskrit Word-Formation*:[10]

In the Pāṇinian tradition we do not find any term for boundary in the sense of pause between two linguistic elements. However, from the various phonological operations based upon the surrounding segments, the role of boundary can be assumed. Joshi S.D has classified them into five, namely, (i) *aṅga* (A.1.4.13); (ii) *pada* (1); (iii) *pada* (2); (A.1.4.14-17); (iv) *bha* (A.1.4.18-20); and (v) *avasāna* (A.1.4.110). These we shall explain as follows:

(i) ***aṅga***: A boundary associated with inflectional or derivational suffix is called *aṅga* and it is marked with '+'. According to Pāṇini, the boundary, namely *aṅga* is that to which a suffix is added[11] and also a stem with a suffix.[12] For example in *bhū* + (*a*), the ū gets *guṇa* (A.7.3.84) as it is an *aṅga*. This results in the formation of the unit *bhava*. The latter becomes an *aṅga* when viewed in relation to the suffix - *mi* which is the first person singular. We have now the form *bhava* + *mi*. Then by the aphorism - *ato dīrgo yañi* (A.7.3.101) the ultimate *a* in *bhava* as *aṅga* gets *dīrgha* resulting in the formation of the word *bhavāmi*.

(ii) ***pada*** (1): A finished word associated with a boundary is called *pada* and can be marked with ' '. The rule *suptiṅantam padam* (*A*.1.4.14) defines *pada* (1) as follows: "that which ends either in *suP* 'case-endings' or *tiṄ* 'finite verb endings' is called *pada*."[13] For example, *rāma* + *sU*. Here the sound *s* in *sU* changes into *ru* when it appears in *pada* boundary, that is, the word-final position. Thus the resultant form is *rāmaḥ*.

(iii) ***pada*** (2): Boundary associated with case-endings and the *taddhita* suffixes beginning with a consonant other than *y* can be termed *pada* (2) and it can be marked with '='. The rule *svādiṣvasarvanāmasthāne* (*A*.1.4.17) defines *pada* (2) as follows: A noun stem acquires the designation of *pada* when it is preceded by the case-endings (*suP*) and the *taddhita* suffixes beginning with a consonant other than *y*. In the case of *suP* we must exclude the suffixes coming under the purview of the *pratyāhāra-suT*.[14] For example, *rājan* = *bhyām*. Here the stem - *rājan* is preceded by a *suP* which is different from *suT* and which begins with the consonant other than *y*. Hence the noun stem-*rājan* acquires the designation of *pada*. And by the operation of the rule *na lopaḥ prātipadikāntasya* (*A*.8.2.7) the sound *n* in *rājan* is dropped.

(iv) ***bha***: A noun stem acquires the designation *bha* when it is preceded by the case-endings (*suP*) which begin with a vowel that does not fall under the purview of the *pratyāhāra* - *suT* and also by the *taddhita*-suffixes that begin with vowels and the consonant *y*.

It can be symbolically represented as " ॥ ". For example, *rājan* ॥ *Jas*. Here the noun-stem-*rājan* has acquired the designation *bha*. It is because it is followed by the suffix *Jas* which falls within *suP* and which begins with the vowel *a*.[15] Then by the operation of the rule - *allopo'naḥ* (*A*. 6.3.134) the *a* of the stem final *an* is dropped. Thus we have the resultant form *rājñaḥ*.

(v) ***avasāna***: A phonetic element whose utterance is not succeeded by any other phonetic element is the ultimate one and it is termed *avasāna*[16] and it can be symbolically represented as ##. For example, the rule *aṇo'pragṛhyasyānunāsikaḥ* (*A*.8.4.59) prescribes the nasalized vowel in the place of ordinary ones, namely, *a, i* and *u* that exist at the *avasāna*-boundary. In the case of *uttamam dadhi, uttamam madhu*, the *i* in *dadhi* and the *u* in *madhu* change into nasalized forms. This rule, however, does not apply at the *pada* boundary, that is, the boundary associated with the word-final position as we find in the case of *madhu bhuṅkte.* Here *u* in *madhu* does not become nasalized in view of the fact that it is not in the *avasāna*-boundary.

Out of these, the *aṅga* (+), the *pada* (1) (#) and the *avasāna* (# #) boundaries occur in all types of word-formations. The remaining two namely, *pada* (2) (=) and *bha* (॥) occur only in respect of case - endings and *taddhita*-suffixes.

From this it follows that as in English, in Sanskrit too, there are some boundary distinctions for various phonological operations. The major distinction between Sanskrit and English boundary is that the boundary in English affects the stress pattern of the base, whereas it does not in Sanskrit. In so far as the TF is concerned, when we look at the boundary level we find *pada* (1) boundary is noticed in the case of application of the *taddhita*-suffixes. However the application of various phonological rules in TF is based upon the remaining four types of boundaries.

2.2. *The Role of Phonology in Taddhita-Formation*

The Role of Phonology in regard to Sanskrit Word-Formation is comparatively very less than that in regard to word-formation in English language. It is because Sanskrit does not have the stress pattern as in English. As pointed out by Bauer L "... English is a relatively complex language, phonologically, speaking with a large number of phonemes and a large amount of phonological variation and alternation. As a result, the problems discussed with relation to English may not occur in other language".[17] Thus it appears that the phonological operation in respect of *Taddhita*-formation is very less because the *Taddhita* suffixes are added to a declined form. Here the phonological operation in regard to the declension of a word takes place even before it acts as a base for the *Taddhita*-formation. It may be added here that the word *samartha* in the aphorism: *samarthānam prathamād vā* (*A*.4.1.82) stands for a word completed in all respects. To quote: *sāmarthyam pariniṣṭhitatvam, kṛtasandhikāryatvam iti yāvat.*[18] In short, *Taddhita*-suffixes do not bring in any drastic change in the body of the words to which they are added, but the phonetic changes which take place in the body of the stem owing to the addition of some specific suffixes are significant.

2.3. We shall now discuss the various phonological operations in regard to TF. To begin with, we shall set forth the classification of phonological operative rules.

WORD-FORMATION RULES AND ADJUSTMENT RULES

2.3.0. *Introduction*

In the process of Word-Formation in Sanskrit we come across two sets of phonological operative rules framed in the *Aṣṭādhyāyī*. One set prescribes the rules necessary for deriving a new word, while another set prescribes specifically some phonological operation and morpho-phonemic changes upon the output. The first group enjoins certain deletions, augmentations and the like alongwith the prescription of Word-Formation Rules (WFRs). The second group prescribes some phonological alternations such as *guṇa, vṛddhi* and the like, and some deletions on the output. The former set of rules may be treated as Word-Formation Rules (WFRs) and the latter as Adjustment Rules (ARs).

2.3.1. *ARs and Taddhita Formation Rules (TFRs)*

In so far as TF is concerned, there are two sets of phonological operative rules, one set which prescribes deletions, etc., and which falls within the sphere of the TF. This set of rules may be termed Internal Phonological Operative Rules (IPOR). Another set which specifies the phonological alternations such as *guṇa*, etc., in the TF are prescribed outside the domain of the *Taddhita*-section in such a manner that they will be applicable to all cases including TF. The reason as to why Pāṇini has included the second set of rules too along with the rules that prescribe phonological operations in all other cases seems to be this: the practical need of this set of rules too, like other phonological operative rules, is the same in this that both alike bring in some phonological changes. Pāṇini must have thought that this second set of rules included within the sphere of the rules that prescribe phonological operations in general may serve as exceptions in so far as the TF is concerned. Thus the phonological rules that are framed outside the domain of *Taddhita* section may be characterised as External Phonological Operative Rules [EPOR].

2.3.1.1. *The Difference Between the Internal and the External Phonological Operative Rules*

The rules we find in the aphorisms beginning with *A*.4.1.76 and ending with *A*.5.4.160 specify certain *Taddhita*-suffixes to be added to the given bases. These suffixes are later deleted leaving the base unchanged. For example, the suffix-*ṭhaK* is added to the base *lavaṇa* and resultant form is *lavaṇa* only meaning that 'which is mixed with salt'. The resultant form should normally be *lāvaṇika* by the application of the substituent rule - *ṭhasyekaḥ* (*A*.7.3.50). But by the application of the specific rule *lavaṇālluk* (*A*.4.4.24) the suffix - *ṭhaK* without making any change to the base undergoes deletion. It must be noted here that the rule that prescribes the deletion of the suffix-*ṭhaK* brings in a change in the meaning of the base without affecting the structure of it.

When we compare this process with the one that falls outside the domain of TF, we find that the resultant form undergoes a change, but the meaning remains to be the same.

For example:

garga	+ *yaÑ*
gārg (ya)	+ *ṄīP*
gārg Ø	+ *ī*
gārgī	

Here there is the deletion of *y* by the rule *halastaddhitasya* (*A*.6.4.150). And, this deletion, unlike the deletion of *ṭhaK* mentioned above, brings in a change in the form of the word only but not in the meaning. This may be the reason for Pāṇini to include the rules like *halastaddhitasya* (*A*.6.4.150) etc., outside the domain of the *Taddhita*-section. And this leads one to assume that according to Pāṇini the rules falling under the TF are different from the rules prescribed elsewhere although the latter are applicable only in TF. We may, therefore, characterise the IPORs as Taddhita-Formation Rules (TFRs) and the other as Adjustment Rules (ARs).

There are, however certain rules within the TFR dealing with phonological changes which resemble ARs. But these are not to be treated as ARs in view of the fact that in these cases the phonological changes are prescribed along with the prescription of a suffix with reference to specific cases. We shall now explain the above two sets of rules in detail.

2.3.2. IPORs function in two ways in regard to TF: (i) by prescribing deletion of certain linguistic elements; and (ii) by predicating certain phonological alternations (*ādeśa-s*) and augments (*āgama-s*) in the bases.

Of these, the first mode is two-fold; as that which brings in phonological deletion in the base, and that which deletes the suffix as such. We shall discuss this in detail now:

2.3.2.1. *Deletions Prescribed with Reference to the Bases*

I. *Rules Enjoining Deletion*	***Deletions***	***Resultant form***
1. sarvtraṆ ca ta lopaśca *A*.4.3.22	heman (ta) + aṆ heman Ø + a	haimanaḥ
2. tadvānamupa° *A*.4.4.125	varcas (vān) + yaT varcas Ø + ya	varcasyaḥ
3. stenādyanna° *A*.5.1.125	ste(na) + yaT ste Ø + ya	steyam
4. tavatithaṃgrahaṇa° *A*.5.2.77	dvi(tīya) + kaN dvi Ø + ka	dvikam
5. vinmatorluk *A*.5:3.65	śrag(vin) + iṣṭhaN śrag Ø + iṣṭha	śragiṣṭhaḥ
6. ajinanta° *A*.5.3.82	vyāghrā(jina) + kaN vyāghra Ø + ka	vyāghrakaḥ

7. thājādūrdhvam° A.5.3.83	deva(datta)+ṭhaC - ika. dev(a) Ø + ika dev Ø + ika	devikaḥ
8. sevala supari° A.5.3.84	sevala(datta)+ ṭha - ika seval(a) Ø + ika seval Ø + ika	sevalikaḥ
9. pādaśatasya° A.5.4.1.	dvipa(a)d+vuṆ dvipa Ø d + aka°	dvipadika
10. arurmana° A.5.4.51.	aru(s) = cvi [19](karoti) aru Ø + Ø karoti	arūkaroti

In the following cases the final *a* is deleted. The rules that prescribe such a deletion belong to the *samāsānta*[20] section of the A.

11. pādasyalopah° A.5.4.138.	vyāghrapād(a) vyāghrapād Ø	vyāghrapāt
12. saṅkhyāsapūrvsya A.5.4.140.	dvipād(a) dvipād Ø	dvipāt
13. kakudasya° A.5.4.146.	ajātakakud(a) ajātakakud Ø	ajātakakut
14. udvibhyām° A.5.4.149.	utkakud(a) utkakud Ø	utkakut

2.3.2.2. *Details of Deletions of the Taddhita Suffixes as such*

By the operation of the rules that prescribe deletions of TS as such, the resultant form retains the form of the base. There is, however, change in the meaning. The process through which the above operation takes place is known as Zero-derivation.[21]

Rules Enjoining Deletion	***Deletion of Suffix***	***Resultant form***
1. dvigorluganapatye A.4.1.88	pañcakapala+aṆ pañcakapāla+Ø	pañcakapālaḥ
2. yūni luk A.4.1.90	gloucukāyana+aṆ gloucukāyana + Ø	gloucukāyanaḥ

3. phak phi	kātya+(phaK-āyana)	kātīyaḥ
N̄oranyatara°	kātya(phaK-āyana)	
A.4.1.91.	+(cha-īya)	
	kātya Ø + īya	
	kāt (ya) + īya	
	kāt Ø + īya	
4. luk striyām	vataṇḍa + (aṆ - a)	vataṇḍī
A.3.1.109	+ (Nin - i)	
	vataṇḍa + Ø when	
	followed by a fem.	
	suffix vataṇḍ Ø = ī	
5. ḍhaki lopaḥ	... pitṛṣvas(ṛ)+	paitṛṣvaseyaḥ
A.4.1.133	(ḍhaK-eya)	
	pitṛṣvas Ø + eya	
	paitṛṣvas+eya	
6. mātṛṣvasuśca	... mātṛṣvas(ṛ) +	mātṛṣvasīyaḥ
A.4.1.134	(chaN-īya)	
	mātṛṣvas Ø + īya	
	mātṛṣvas + īya	
7. kambojālluk	... kamboja+aÑ-a	kambojaḥ
A.4.1.175	kamboja + Ø	
8. striyāmavanti -	... avanti + (ÑyaṄ - ya)	
kunti kurubhyaśca	+ ṄīṢ - ī	
A.4.1.176	kunti + (ÑyaṄ - ya)+	
	(ṄīṢ - ī)	
	kuru + (Ñya-ya)	
	+ūṄ - ū)	
	avanti + Ø + ī	avantī
	kunti + Ø + ī	kuntī
	kuru + Ø + ū	kurūḥ
	Ø when followed	
	by a fem. suffix.	
9. lubaviśeṣa	... (adya) puṣya + aṆ	(adya)puṣyaḥ
A.4.2.4.	(adya) pusya + Ø	
10. samjñāyām	... sravaṇā + aṆ	
śravaṇāśvattha -	asvattha+aṆ	
bhyām.	sravaṇa + Ø	śravaṇā
A.4.2.65	aśvattha+ Ø	aśvatthaḥ

11. prokttāl luk A.4.2.68	... pāṇinīya+aṆ pāṇinīya+Ø	pāṇinīyam
12. sūtrācca kopadhāt A.4.2.65	aṣṭakā+aṆ aṣṭakā+Ø	aṣṭakā
13. janapade lup A.4.2.81	... pañcāla+aṆ pañcāla+Ø	pancālāḥ
14. varaṇādibhyaśca A.4.2.82	... varaṇā+aṆ varaṇā + Ø	varanāḥ
15. śarkarāyāvā A.4.2.83	... śarkarā+aṆ śarkarā + Ø	śarkarā
16. śraviṣṭhāphalguny° A.4.3.34.	... śraviṣṭhā+aṆ śraviṣṭhā + Ø	śraviṣṭhāḥ, etc.
17. sthānāntagośāla° A.4.3.35	... gosthāna+aṆ gosthāna+Ø	gosthānaḥ, etc.
18. vatsaśālābhiji° A.4.3.36	... vatsaśāla+aṆ vatsaśāla + Ø	vatsaśālaḥ, etc.
19. nakṣtrebhyo bahulam A.4.3.37	rohiṇī+aṆ rohiṇī + Ø	rohiṇaḥ, etc.
20. kaṭhacarakāḷḷuk A.4.3.107	kaṭha+ṆiN kaṭha+Ø	kaṭhaḥ, etc.
21. phale luk A.4.3.163	amalakīm+ṆiN āmalakī+Ø	āmalakam
22. lup ca A.4.3.167	jambu+Mayaṭ jambu+Ø	jambūḥ
23. harītakyādibhyaśca A.4.3.167	harītakī+aṆ harītakī+Ø	harītakyaḥ
24. kaṁsīya° A.4.3.168	kaṁsīya+yaÑ kaṁsīya+Ø	kaṁsīyam
25. lavaṇālluk A.4.4.24	lavaṇa+ṭhaK lavaṇa+Ø	lavaṇaḥ
26. madhorñaca A.4.4.29	madhu+Ña madhu+Ø	madhuḥ
27. ekadhurāllukecā A.4.4.79	ekadhura+kha ekadhura+Ø	ekadhuraḥ
28. adhyardha° A.5.1.28	adhyardhakaṁsa +kaN adhyardhakaṁsa+Ø	adhyardha- kaṁsam
29. vibhāṣākarṣā° A.5.1.29	adhyardhakārṣā- paṇa+TiṬHaN adhyardha-kārṣāpaṇa+Ø	adhyardhakār- ṣāpāṇam

30. dvitripūrvā° *A*.5.1.30	dviniṣka+ThaÑ dviniṣka+Ø	dviniṣkam
31. bistācca *A*.5.1.31	dvibista+ṭhaÑ dvibista+Ø	dvibistam
32. kulijālluk khauca *A*.5.1.55	dvikuluja+ṭhaN dvikulija+Ø	dvikulijī
33. varsālluk ca[22] *A*.5.1.88	dvivarṣa+kha dvivarṣa+Ø	dvivarṣaḥ
34. adhyāyānuvāka-yorluk *A*.5.2.60	gardabhāṇḍa+Cha gardabhāṇḍa+Ø	gardabhāṇḍaḥ
35. añcerluk *A*.5.3.30	prācī+astāti prācī+Ø	prācī
36. mānapasvaṅgayoḥ *A*.5.3.51	aṣṭama+Ña aṣṭama+Ø	aṣṭamaḥ
37. ekādākiniccā sahāye *A*.5.3.52	eka+kam eka+Ø	ekaḥ
38. lummanuṣye *A*.5.3.98	cañcā+kaN cancā+Ø	cancā
39. jīvikārthecāpaṇye *A*.5.3.99	vāsudeva+kaN vāsudeva+Ø	vāsudevaḥ
40. devapathādi-bhyaśca *A*.5.3.100	devapatha+kaN devapatha+Ø	devapathaḥ, etc.

So far we have discussed the IPORs which function by prescribing deletions of the TSs. Now we shall discuss the same rules which function by predicating phonological alternations [*ādeśa*] and augments [*āgama*] to the base.

2.3.2.3. *Phonological Alternations Prescribed to the base*

1. maturutsaṁkhyā *A*.4.1.115	sammat(ṛ)+ aṆ sāmmat(ur)+*a* sāmmatur+*a*	sāmmāturaḥ
2. kanyāyāḥ kanīna ca *A*.4.1.116	(kanyā)+aṆ kanīna+*a* kānīna+*a*	kānīnaḥ
3. sudhāturakaṄ ca *A*.4.1.97	sudhāt(ṛ)+ iÑ sudhāt(aka) + i saudhātaka+i	saudhātakiḥ

4.	kalyāṇyādīnāminaṆ *A*.4.1.126	kalyāṇ(T)+dhak-(eya) kalyāṇ(inaṅ)+eya kālyāṇīna+eya	kālyāṇineyaḥ
5.	kulaṭāyā vā[23] *A*.4.1.127	kulaṭ(ā)+ḍhaK-(eya) kulaṭ(inaṄ)+ eya kaulaṭina+eya	kaulaṭineyaḥ
6.	rājñaḥka ca *A*.4.2.140	rāja(n)+cha-(īya) rāja(K)+iya	rājakīyam
7.	tavakamamakā-vekavacane *A*.4.3.3	(i) (yuṣmad)+khaN-(ina) tāvaka+īna	tāvakīnaḥ
		(ii) (asmad)+khaN-(ina) māmaka+īna	māmakīnaḥ
8.	pathaḥ pantha ca *A*.4.3.29	(patha)+vuN-(aka) (pantha)+aka	panthakaḥ
9.	treḥ samprasāraṇam ca *A*.5.2.55	t(ri)+tīya t(ṛ)+tīya	tṛtīyaḥ
10.	idama iś *A*.5.3.3	(idam)+tasīL (iŚ)+tas i+tas.	itaḥ
11.	etadoN *A*.5.3.5	(etad)+tasiL aN+tas a+tas	ataḥ
12.	sarvasya so'nya-tarasyam° *A*.5.3.6	(sarva)+dā sa+dā	sadā
13.	uparyupariṣṭāt *A*.5.3.31	(ūrdhva)+riL upa+ri	upari
14.	paścāt *A*.5.3.32	(apara)+ātI paśca+āt	paścāt
15.	pūrvādhara° *A*.5.3.39	(pūrva)+astātI pur+astāt	purastāt
16.	praśasyasyaśraḥ *A*.5.3.60	praśasya+iṣṭhaN śra+iṣṭha	śreṣṭhaḥ
17.	jya ca *A*.5.3.61	(praśasya)+iṣṭhaN jya+iṣṭha	jyeṣṭhaḥ

18. vṛddhasya ca	(vṛddha)+iṣṭhaN	
A.5.3.62	jya+iṣṭha	jyeṣṭhaḥ
19. antikabādha°	(antika)+iṣṭhaN	
A.5.3.63	ned(a)+iṣṭha	
	ned Ø + iṣṭha	nediṣṭhaḥ
20. yuvālpayoḥ...	yuva+iṣṭhaN	
A.5.3.64	kan+iṣṭha	kaniṣṭhaḥ
21. kasya ca daḥ	dhak+akaC	
A.5.3.72	dhak+i(k)	
	dhaki+d	dhakit
22. ahnorhna ete-bhyaḥ	dvi+(ahan)	
	dv(i)+ahna	
A.5.4.88	dvyahna	dvyahnaḥ
23. prasaṁbhyām	pra+(jānu)	
A.5.4.129	pra+jñu	prajñuḥ
24. ūdhaso'naṄ; dhanuṣaśca	dvi+dhanu(s)	
	dvi+dhanu anaṆ	
A.5.4.131-132	dvi+dhan(u)an	
	dvi+dhanv an	dvidhānvā
25. jāyāyā niṆ	yuvati+jāy(a)	
A.5.3.134	yuvati+jay niṅ	
	yuvati+jā(y)ni	
	yuvati+jā Ø ni	
	yuva(ti) + jāni	
	yuva Ø + jāni	yuvajāniḥ
26. ekasya sakṛcca	(eka) + suC	
A.5.4.19	sakṛt+Ø	sakṛt
27. gandhasyet°	ut+gandh(a)	
A.5.4.135	u(t)gandh(i)	
	udgandhi	udgandhiḥ
28. vayasi dantasya°	dvi+(danta)	
A.5.4.141	dvi+datṚ	
	dvi+dat	
	dvi+danUMt	
	dvi+dan(t)	
	dvi+dan Ø	dvidan

2.3.2.4. *Augmentation Prescribed to the Base*

Rules prescribing augmentation	***Augments***	***Resultant Form***
1. manorjātā ...	manu+yaT	
A.4.1.161	manu(ṣUK)+ya	
	manu(ṣ)+ya	manuṣyaḥ
2. naḍādīnām kuk ca	naḍa+cha-īya	
A.4.2.91	naḍa(kUK)+īya	
	naḍa(k)+īya	naḍakīyaḥ
3. sāyam ciram ...	sāyam+Tyu-ana	
A.4.3.23	sāyam(tUṬ)+ana	
	sāyam(t) + ana	sāyamtanam
4. trapujatunch ṣUK	trapu+aN	
A.4.3.138	trapu(ṣUK)+a	
	trāpu(ṣ) + a	trāpuṣam
5. vātātisarabhyam	vāta+iNI	
kUK ca	vata(kUK) + i	
A.5.2.129	vāta(k)+i	vātakī

To sum up this part of the discussion: IPORs prescribe deletions of linguistic elements in certain cases and also phonological alternatives in and augments to the base.

We shall now deal with the External Phonological Operative Rules.

2.4. EPORs function on the basis of *iT* or indicatory letters. Hence we shall first discuss the role of *iT* in TF.

2.4.0. *The Role of iT-s or Indicatory Letteis in TF*

Certain Phonological Operations proceed on the basis of several *iT* sounds or indicatory letters. There are three major functions of *iT*-s; and, they are:

(a) facilitation of the pronunciation of the suffixes such as *i* and *u* (*uccāranārthaḥ*). For example, the final letter *i* added to the suffix *iNI* facilitates the pronunciation of suffixes. The *iTs* have no other function apart from this;

(b) indication or specification of the accents. For example, *c, t, p,* etc. indicate different accents such as *antodātta, svarita,* etc.,[24] and

(c) indication of the phonological changes such as *vṛddhi*, etc., that take place in the base as well as in the output.

The present section is devoted to the discussion on the last item.

The vowels *i* and *u*, and the consonants *k, c, ñ, ṭ, ḍ, ṇ, t, n, p, r, l, ṣ* and *s* have been used as *iTs* or indicatory letters alongwith the *Taddhita*-suffixes. These have been used individually as well as jointly, but the function of each one is clearly demarcated. The change that is brought in by the above *iTs* in the base as well as in the output varies in the case of the functioning of each *iT*. It should be noted here that several suffixes would appear to be identical (*sarūpa*) when divested of their *iTs* or indicatory letters. For example, the suffix - *aṆ* and - *aÑ* would appear to be the same when the *iTs* are deleted. Though in actual usage they are the same, yet the phonological changes undergone by the bases vary. The difference in the *iTs* or indicatory letters clearly point out the grammatical changes, if any, that the base and the suffix undergo. Thus, as in other cases, in *TF* also the *iTs* or indicatory letters present in the *Taddhita*-suffixes play a vital role in regard to the phonological changes.

2.4.1. *External Phonological Operative Rules*

2.4.1.0. There are two types of External Phonological Operative Rules in regard to the TF. One is the phonological alternations such as *guṇa, vṛddhi* and the like and another, the deletion of certain linguistic elements.

2.4.1. *Phonological Alternations*

2.4.1.1. *Guṇa*: The Final *u* attains *guṇa* by the operation of the rule *orguṇaḥ* (A.6.4.146) as in the case of *aupagavaḥ*:

(u) *pagu* + *aṆ*
aupag (u) + *a*
aupag (o) + *a*
aupagav + *a*
aupagava.

2.4.1.2. *Vṛddhi*: The initial vowel of the base attains *vṛddhi* by the operation of the rule *taddhiteṣvacāmādeḥ* (A.7.2.117) when followed by the *Taddhita*-suffixes - *Ñit, Ṇit* and *Kit* as in the case of *aupagavaḥ*:

(u) *pagu + aṆ*
aupago + a - aupagava.

In must be noted here that this rule is a general one. This is superseded by the rules beginning with *A*.7.3.1. and ending with *A*.7.3.31 which prescribe in the bases certain phonological changes which are different from *vṛddhi*. For example, the rule - *na yvābhyām padāntābhyām pūrvautu tābhyāmaiC* (*A*.7.3.3) does not prescribe *vṛddhi* for the initial vowel of the base, but the augments *ai* and *au* in respect of the bases that end with *y* and *v*. In the case of *vaiyākaraṇaḥ* :

vyākaraṇa + aṆ
v(ai)yākaraṇa + a
vaiyākaraṇa + a - vaiyākaraṇaḥ

Thus the phonological operation of *vṛddhi* prescribed by the rule *A*.7.2.117 is negatived by the rules that extend upto *A*.7.3.31.

2.4.1.3. *Dīrgha*

The ultimate vowel of the base is lengthened when the suffix *cvi* is followed as in the case of *śucībhavati*:

śuci + cvi (bhavati)
śucī + Ø bhavati
śucībhavati.

2.4.2. *Deletions*

Deletions of certain linguistic elements in the process of TF may be classified into three types, namely, the Truncation of case-endings, deletion of the *Taddhita*-suffixes in a specific environment and the deletion of some elements in the output.

2.4.2.1. *Rules That Prescribe Truncation*

In Sanskrit Word-Formation, suffixes are added either to a word or to a stem, or to a root. In this regard the *Taddhita*-suffixes are mostly added to a nominal word.[25] When the suffixcs arc added to a given word there is a truncation of the case-ending which is a part of the base. Such kind of deletion takes place wherever a word which consists of a stem + suffix acts as a base. This may be formulated as follows:

(stem + suffix) # suffix (Derivational) (stem) + Ø + suffix

For example,

(*daśaratha* + *Ṅas)* # *iÑ*

St Suf

(daśaratha)$_{st}$+ Ø + *i*

(dāśarathi)$_{st}$

Here the genitive case-ending, namely, + *Ṅas* is deleted by the operation of the rule *supodhātuprātipadikayoḥ* (*A*.2.4.71).

2.4.2.2. *Deletion of the Taddhita-Suffixes in Specific Instances*

Deletion of certain phonological elements has been prescribed in the *aṅgādhikāra* and also in the aphorisms beginning with *A*.2.4.62 and ending with *A*.2.4.70 in the 4th chapter of the 2nd *adhyāya* which does not consist of the IPORs. We shall take the latter for discussion herein.

Deletion of the *Taddhita*-suffixes prescribed in the Fourth Chapter of the Second *adhyāya* in the aphorisms beginning with *A*.2.4.62 to 2.4.70 takes place under the following conditions:

1. the resultant form must be plural in number;
2. it must not be a feminine gender word; and
3. it should not form part of a compound-word.[26]

For example, the word *aṅgāḥ*. It is derived thus:

(*aṅga* + *am*) *aṆ* (*Jas*)

(*aṅga*) + Ø + *aṆ* (*Jas*)

(*aṅga*) Ø (*Jas*) - *aṅgāḥ*

Here the word *aṅgāḥ* which is a resultant form of the derivation is not a feminine gender word; nor does it form *part of a compound* word. It is plural in number. Hence the *Taddhita*-suffix - *aṆ* is deleted on the basis of this rule (*A*.2.4.62). These conditions are extended upto the rule *A*.2.4.70.

This type of deletion appears to be similar to the one that is brought about by the operation of the IPORs. But there is a difference between the two in this that the deletion caused by the IPORs, unlike the one that is caused by EPORs is not limited by the three conditions outlined above. In other words, the IPORs are unconditional whereas the EPORs are conditional.

The Aphorisms beginning with *A*.2.4.62 and ending with *A*.2.4.70 prescribe the deletion of *Taddhita*-suffixes under the three conditions mentioned above. We shall deal with this now.

The *Gotra*-Suffix which is added to the bases *yaska,* etc. is deleted by the operation of the rule *yaskādibhyo gotre* (*A*.2.4.63). For example:

yaska + aṆ (Jas)
yaska + Ø (Jas)
yaskāḥ

The *Gotra*-Suffixes - *yaÑ* and - *ā* which are added to the bases such as *garga, bida,* etc., are deleted by the operation of the rule *yaÑaÑośca* (*A*.2.4.64).

For example:

garga + yaÑ (Jas)
garga + (Jas)
gargāḥ

The *Gotra*-suffixes - *ḍhak* etc., which are added to the base such as *atri,* etc., are deleted by the operation of the rule *atribṛgu*°.. (*A*.2.4.65).

For example:

atri + ḍhak (Jas)
atri + Ø (Jas)
atrayaḥ

The *Gotra*-suffix - *iÑ* which is added to a poly-syllabic word when the *gotra* people called *prācya* (Eastern) and *bharata* are denoted is deleted by the operation of the rule *bahvacaḥ*°.. (*A*.2.4.66)

pannāgāra + iÑ (Jas)
pannāgāra + Ø (Jas)
pannāgāraḥ

The *Gotra*-suffixes such as - *phiÑ,* etc., which are added to the words such as *taikāyani,* and *kaitavayni* that are derived from words *tika* and *kitava* respectively are deleted by the operation of the rule *tikakitava°..* (*A*.2.4.68) when these two words are united together to form a *dvandva* compound.

For example:

tika + phiÑ - taikāyani
kitva + phiÑ - kaitavāyani
(taikāyanaśca kaitavāyanaśca)
tika + phiÑ + (Jas) + kitava + phiÑ + (Jas)
tika + Ø+ kitava + Ø
tikakitavāḥ

The *Gotra*-suffix *phaK* which is added to words such as *upakalamakāḥ* that are compound words of *dvandva* type is deleted optionally by the operation of the rule *upakādi°..* (*A*.2.4.69)

For example:

(i) *upaka + phaK - aupakāyana*
lamaka + phaK - lāmakāyana
aupakāyanaśca lāmakāyanaśca
upaka + phaK + (Jas) + lamaka + phaK + (Jas)
upaka + Ø + lamaka + Ø
upakalamakāḥ

Optional Form :

(ii) *aupakāyanalāmakāyanāḥ* :

It must be noted here that this rule is applicable in the case of words *upaka* and *lamaka* also when they are used independently.

For example:

(i) *upaka + phaK + (Jas)*
upaka + Ø (Jas)
upakāḥ

(ii) *Optional Form* :
upaka + phaK - āyana + Jas
upaka + āyana (Jas)
upakāyanāḥ

Exactly similar consideration applies to the word *lamaka* too.

The suffixes such as - *aṆ*, etc., which are added to the bases *āgastya*, etc., are deleted by the operation of the rule *āgastya°..*

(*A*.2.4.70). The form *āgastya* which remains after the deletion of the *Taddhita*-suffix will be replaced by the word *agasti*.

For example:

āgastya + aṆ (Jas)
āgastya + Ø (Jas)
agasti + as - agastayaḥ

2.4.2.3. The deletions that are prescribed outside the domain of the *Taddhita*-section but enjoined within the *aṅgādhikāra* will be explained in this section. In the following cases the deletion takes place accordingly.

(1) The final *n* of the base is deleted by the operation of the rule *nastaddhite* (*A*.6.4.144).

For example:

agniśarmaṇ + iÑ
āgniśarm(an) + i
āgniśarm ø + i
āgniśarmiḥ

(2) The ultimate vowels, namely, *a* and *i* of the bases are deleted by the rule *yasyeti ca* (*A*.6.4.148). For example:

daśaratha + iÑ
dāśarath(a) + i
dāśarath Ø + i
dāśarathiḥ

(3) The vowel *u* of the base is deleted when it is followed by a suffix beginning with *ḍh* by the rule *ḍhe lopo'kadravāḥ* (*A*.6.4.147). For example:

kamaṇḍalu + ḍhak - eya
kāmaṇḍal (u) + eya
kāmaṇḍal Ø + eya
kāmaṇḍaleyaḥ

(4) The consonant *y* of the *Taddhita*-suffix that is added to bring out the sense of 'one's offspring' is deleted by the rule *halastaddhitasya* (*A*.6.4.150) when it is followed by the vowel *i*.

For example:

gārg (ya) + ṄīP
gārg Ø + ī
gārgī

(5) The consonant *y* of the *Taddhita*-suffix which is added to bring out the sense of 'one's offspring' is deleted by the rule *āpatyasyacataddhite'nāti* (*A*.6.4.151), when it is followed by an another *Taddhita*-suffix other than *ā*.

For example:

gārg(ya) + cha - īya

gārg Ø + īya

gārgīya

(6) The consonant *y* of the *Taddhita*-suffix which is added to bring out the sense of 'one's offspring' is deleted by the rule *kyacvyośca* (*A*.6.4.152) when it is followed by the suffixes *kya* and *cvi*.

For example:

gārg (ya) + cvi (bhavati)

gārg Ø + Øbhavati

gārgī + bhavati

gārgībhavati

(7) The suffix *cha* is deleted in respect of the words which are listed under *bilvaka* group by the rule *bilvakādibhyaścha* (*A*.6.4.153) when it is followed by an another *Taddhita*-suffix.

For example:

bilvaka + cha - īya + aṆ

bailvaka + Ø + a

bailvakaḥ

(8) The letter *tṛ* of the base is deleted by the rule *turiṣṭhemeyassu* (*A*.6.4.154) when it is followed by the suffixes, namely, *iṣṭhan, iman, īyas.*

For example:

kar (tṛ) + iṣṭhaN

kar Ø + iṣṭha

kariṣṭhaḥ

(9) The *ṭi* part[27] of the base is deleted when it is followed by the suffixes *iṣṭhaN*, etc.

For example:

paṭ (u) + iṣṭhaN

paṭ Ø + iṣṭha

paṭiṣṭhaḥ

(10) The *yaṆ* [*y, v, r, l*] which is part of the base is deleted by the rule *sthūladūra°* (*A*.6.4.156) when it is followed by the suffixes *iṣṭhaN* and the vowel preceded by the *yaṆ* gets the *guṇa* too. For example:

sthū (la) + iṣṭhaN
sthū Ø + iṣṭha
sth (ū) + iṣṭha
sth (ū) + iṣṭha
sthav + iṣṭha
sthaviṣṭhaḥ

(11) The vowel *i* of the suffix *īyas* is deleted and the base bahu is altered into *bhū* by the rule *bahorlopo°* (*A*.6.4.158).

For example:

bahu + (ī) yas
(bahu) + Ø yas
bhū + yas
bhūyaḥ

(12) The vowel *i* of the suffix *iṣṭhaN* is deleted and the base *bahu* is altered into *bhū* and the augment *yiT* is added by the rule *iṣṭhasya yiṭ ca* (*A*.6.1.159) For example:

bahu + (i) ṣṭhaN
(bahu) + Ø ṣṭha
bhū yiṬ + ṣṭa
bhūyiṣṭhaḥ

2.5. *Phonologically Conditioned Taddhita-Suffixes*

2.5.0. The *Taddhita*-suffixes are morphologically classified under six headings. Each one of these consists of several types of suffixes. For example, the general suffix - *aṆ* is a major morphological domain (*aṆ-adhikāra*). This includes a number of suffixes which are enjoined for specific bases or particular environments. A detailed account of the above classification will be dealt with in the next chapter. The present section deals with the description of some specific *Taddhita*-suffixes prescribed for phonologically conditioned bases as could be noticed in the *A*.

2.5.1. *Various Phonological Features*

The various phonological features such as (1) stem finals, (2) accent, (3) syllable constituency, (4) structure of initial syllable (*vṛddha*), and (5) nature of penultimate sound (*upadhā*) govern some of the *Taddhita*-suffixes. These are however, exceptions to some other suffixes within different domains. We shall now explain each Phonological feature along with the suffixes that are conditioned by the same.

2.5.1. *Stem Final as Conditional Feature*

The following are the suffixes which are conditioned by some vowels in the stem finals:

In the following cases, the symbols → and ∠ signify exception and condition respectively.

	Rule	**Suffix**	**Example**
1.	ata iÑ *A*.4.1.95	aṆ→i ∠ Na	dāśārathiḥ, etc.
2.	ata ini ṭhaNau *A*.5.2.115	matuP→i and ṬhaN ∠ Na	daṇḍī, daṇḍikaḥ
3.	itaścāniñaḥ *A*.4.1.122	aṆ → DhaK (eya) ∠ Ni	dauleyaḥ
4.	OraÑ *A*.4.2.71	aṆ → aÑ ∠ Nu	kākṣatavam
5.	OrdeśethaÑ *A*.4.2.119	aṆ → thaÑ (ika) ∠ Nu	naiṣāda karṣūḥ
6.	OraÑ *A*.4.3.139	aṆ → aÑ ∠ Nu	daivadāravam
7.	ṛtaṣṭhaÑ *A*.4.3.78	aṆ → thaÑ(ika) ∠ Nṛ	hautṛkam
8.	rtoraÑ *A*.4.4.49	ṭhak (ika) → aÑ ∠ Nṛ	yātram
9.	ṛtoraṆ *A*.5.1.105	thaÑ (ika) → aṆ ∠ Nṛ	ārtavam
10.	igantācca laghupūrvāt *A*.5.1.131	tva / taL → aṆ ∠ Nik[28]	maunam, etc.

2.5.2. *Accent as Conditional Feature*

There are some TS exclusively applied to bases having *anudātta* accent on the first syllable. These are as follows:

Rule	*Sufix*	*Example*
1. anudāttāderaÑ A.4.2.44	aṆ - aÑ / N having anudātta accent on the first syllable	kāpotam, etc.
2. anudāttādeśca A.4.3.140	- do -	dādhittham, etc.

2.5.3. *Syllabic Constituency as Conditional Feature*

Rule	*Suffix*	*Example*
1. dvyacaḥ A.4.1.121	aṆ - ḍhaK (eya)/N having disyllabic feminine gender	dātteyaḥ
2. aṆo dvyacaḥ A.4.1.156	iÑ-[29] phiN(ayana)/N having disyllabic word	kārtrāyaṇiḥ[30]
3. dvyacaḥ chandasi[31] A.4.3.150	aṆ - mayaṬ/N having disyllabic word	parṇamayī
4. baḥvaco'ntodāttāt	aṆ - ThaÑ (ika) / N having poly-syllabic bases coupled with the feature of udātta accent on the final syllable	ṣātvaṇatvikaḥ, etc.
5. bahvacaḥkūpeṣu A.4.2.73	aṆ - aÑ / N having poly-syllabic word when the output refers to 'a well'.[32]	dairghavaratraḥ (kūpaḥ)

2.5.4. *Structure of Initial Syllable*

The bases called *vṛddha*[33] constitute a distinct group for the addition of TS:

Rule	Suffix	Example
1. vṛddhāṭṭhaK[34] *A.*4.1.148	aṆ-ṭhaK(ika)/N bases having the designation *vṛddha*	bhāgavittikaḥ
2. vṛddhācchaḥ *A.*4.2.114	aN-cha(iya)/N bases having the designation *vṛddha*	śālīyaḥ, etc.
3. vṛddhātprācām *A.*4.2.120	aṆ-thaÑ(ika)/N bases having the designation *vṛddha*	āḍhakajambukaḥ
4. vṛddhādaka° *A.*4.2.141	aṆ-Cha(iya)/N bases having the designation *vṛddha*	brāḥmaṇakīyaḥ

2.5.5. *Changes caused by Penultimate Sound* [*Upadhā*]:

The bases having the penultimate sound such as *k, y,* etc. form a group for addition of the TS:

Rule	Suffix	Example
1. kopadhācca *A.*4.2.79	aÑ-aṆ/N[35] bases having *k* as penultimate sound	traiśaṅkavam
2. kopadhādaṆ *A.*4.2.132	VuÑ-aN/N[36] bases having *k* as penultimate sound	ārṣikaḥ
3. kopadhācca *A.*4.3.137	aÑ-aṆ/N[37] bases having *k* as penultimate sound	tārkavam
4. yopadhāt° *A.*5.1.132	tva/taL - VuÑ(aka)/N bases having *y* as penultimate sound and preceded by a prosodically long sound.	rāmaṇīyakam

2.6. *Accentual Variations due to the Addition of Taddhita-Suffixes*

2.6.0. Like other phonological changes effected by the phonological operation such as *guṇa, vṛddhi,* etc., there is accentual variation effected by the phonological operation of the TS. Now we shall discuss some accentual variations owing to the addition of the TS.

2.6.1. Earlier we have referred to the role of the *iT*-s or indicatory letters in suffixes.[38] There are many TSs which contain the indicatory letters; and their purpose is varied. But the suffixes with the indicatory letters, *K, C, Ñ, T, N, P, R,* and *L* have the function of effecting changes in the accent too in the resultant forms. We shall record the individual cases wherein accentual variations take place by the addition of the suffixes having these indicatory letters.

K. The indicatory letter *K* points out that by the addition of the *Kit* suffixes the resultant form gets the *antodātta*[39] accent as in the case of *yadāgneyaḥ.* There are twelve TSs which have *k* as *iT.* They are: *āraK, airaK, kaK, ṭhaK, ḍhaK, ḍhinuK, ḍraK, tyaK, phaK, yaK, vuK,* and *ṢpaK.*

C. This indicates that the new words which are effected by the addition of *cit* suffixes get the *antodātta*[40] accent. There are nearly fifty suffixes having this indicatory letter. Some of them are: *akaC, athaC, adaC, atasuC, asiC, akikaC, āṭaC, iC, itaC, uraC,* etc.

Ñ. A TS with *Ñ* as an *anubandha,* indicates the *antodātta*[41] accent would fall on the first syllable of the derived word. They are nearly twenty suffixes which have *Ñ* as *iT.* They are : *aÑ, iÑ, ukaÑ, khaÑ, cphaÑ, Ñith, Ñya, ÑyaÑ, ÑyaT, ḍhakaÑ, dhaÑ, naÑ, phaÑ, phiÑ, yaÑ, vuÑ, ṣyaÑ, ṣlaÑ* and *snaÑ.*

T. T as *iT* in the TS indicates that the word derived by the addition of this suffix would get the *svarita* accent[42] on its final syllable. The letter T is *iT* in the TS, namely, *DyaT, ṆyaT, VyaT* and *yaT.*

N. The *N* used as *i* indicates the *antodātta* accent[43] on the initial syllable of the new word. Twenty TSs have *N* as *anubandha* and they are as follows: *aN, iṣṭhaN, īkaN, iyasuN, iraN, kaN, ghaN, tithaN, DyuN, thaN, tikaN, thaN, tyakaN, thyaN, PhiN, yaN, VyuN, SakaN* and *ṢthaN.*

P. The presence of *P* as *anubandha* in any suffix indicates that the suffix causes the *anudātta* accent.[44] The suffixes having *P* as *iT* are as follows: *enaP, kalpaP, kunaP, CṇaP, cuñcuP, ThaP, ḌmatuP, tamaP, tayaP, taraP, tyaP, pāśaP, matuP, maP, yaP, rūpaP* and *vatuP*.

R. There are only two TSs *jātīyaR* and *deśiyaR* having *R* as their indicatory letters. The presence of *R* in a suffix indicates that the words formed by the addition of such suffixes will have an acute accent on the penultimate syllable.[45]

L. *L* as an indicatory letter is found in twelve TS; and it is indicative of the *udātta* accent[46] on the syllable immediately preceding it. In other words, the *Lit* suffixes, when added to the base having *antodātta* accent would change the resultant form into one having *udātta* accent in the ultimate syllable. The following are the TSs having the *L* as their indicatory letter: *ṬyuL, taL, taṣiL, tātiL, tiL, traL, thaL, bhaktaL, yaL, rihaL, vidyaL* and *ṢṭhaL*.

To sum up

An analysis of the Phonological Features involved in the process of the derivation of new words by the addition of TS has led us to identify two types of phonological operative rules, namely, IPOR which are prescribed within the sphere of the *Taddhita*-section and EPOR which falls outside its domain. The former set of rules is treated as TFRs and the latter as ARs. We have also identified certain suffixes which are prescribed as exceptions to the suffixes enjoined in a general manner. The addition of these suffixes are conditioned by the Phonological factors such as stem finals, accent, syllable constituency and the like. We have also discussed on accentual variations due to the addition of some suffixes.

In the following chapter, we shall deal with the Morphological Features relating to the TF.

REFERENCES

1. Aronoff M., *Word-Formation in Generative Grammar*, p. 63.
2. *Topics in English Derivational Morphology*.
3. *Morphological Investigations*.
4. *Sound Pattern in English*.

5. *Topics in English Derivational Morphology.*
6. *Morphological Investigations.*
7. These examples are taken from Bauer, L., *Introducing Linguistic Morphology.*
8. *Ibid.*
9. See Chomsky and Halle, SPE; Siegel, *Topics in English Derivational Morphology*; Aronoff, *Word-Formation in Generative Grammar*; Allen, *Morphological Investigations;* Kiparsky, *Lexical Morphology* and *Phonology*; Selkirk, *Syntax of Words*; Bauer, L., *Introducing Linguistic Morphology*; and Phillip Kar, *Phonology* for detailed discussion.
10. The present section gives a brief account on the different types of boundaries occurring in the *Aṣṭādhyāyī*. For details see Joshi, S.D. *Amṛtadhāra* pp. 181-186.
11. *yasmād pratyayavidhiḥ tadaṅgam.*
12. *tadādipratyaye tadaṅgam.*
13. *subantam tiNantam ca pada samjñam syāt.* *SK.* on *A.*1.1.14.
14. *suṬ* is the *pratyāhāra* comprising of the three case-endings of the nominative case and the singular and the dual number of the accusative case. This *suT-pratyāhāra* added to the masculine and the feminine gender stems is technically termed *sarvanāmasthāna.* And the same added to the neuter gender stem is not designated so and is therefore excluded in the present case.
15. In *Jas* the sound *J* is dropped by the operation of the rules - *cuṭū* (*A.*1.3.7) and *tasyalopaḥ* (*A.*1.3.8).
16. *varṇānāmabhāvaḥ avasāna saṁjñaṁ syāt, SK.* on *A.*1.4.110.
17. *English Word-Formation*, p. 101.
18. *SK* on *A.*4.1.82.
19. This suffix as such is deleted (*sarvalopī pratyayaḥ*).
20. *samāsānta* is a sub-section of the *Taddhita*-section of the *Aṣṭādhyāyī* which sets forth the suffixes that can be added to the compound bases.
21. Allan K. defines the zero derivation as follows: "With zero derivation, a zero affix attaches to an existing lexeme, causing it to shift its lexical class, thus to become a different lexeme" (*Linguistic meaning* Vol. I, p. 217). For details see also Marchand, *The Categories and Types of Present Day English Word-Formation*; Adams, *An Introduction to English Word-Formation*; Aronoff, *Word-Formation in Generative Grammar*;

Bauer, *English Word-Formation; and Introducing Linguistic Morphology*.

22. Here from the particle *ca* we get the alternative forms, namely, *dvivarṣikaḥ* and *dvivarṣīṇaḥ* by the addition of the suffixes - *ṭhaÑ* and *kha* respectively.
23. The alternative form is derived thus:
 k(u)laṭā + ḍhaK - (eya)
 kaulaṭā + eya
 kaulaṭeyaḥ
24. A detailed account on accentual variations that take place because of *iT*-s will be discussed in the following section.
25. The TS-s which fall under the category of *atyantasvārthika*-type are added not to a word but to a nominal stem (*prātipadika*).
26. *tadrājasya bahuṣu tenaivāstriyām* (A.2.4.62).
27. A.1.1.64.
28. Here the word *ik* stands for the vowels *i, u, r* and *l*.
29. This is an exception to the rule that prescribes the suffix - *aṆ* in a general manner.
30. Here the word *kartra* is the base which is a disyllabic word and which has - *aṆ* at its end. The suffix - *aṆ* is added to the base *kartṛ* to bring out the sense of 'one's disciple', etc., by the rule A.4.4.120.
31. In the section that comes under the heading *bhāṣāyām* the rule *mayaT vetaiyoḥ°* A.4.3.143. prescribes the suffix - *mayaṬ* will, therefore, be applicable to words in classical language and not to those in Vedic one. But it should apply to the latter also. For this, the present rule is enjoined.
32. This is also a semantically conditioned TS.
33. The bases which are having the vowels bearing the appellation *vṛddhi* in the initial position are designated as *vṛddha*. vide: *vṛddhiryasyacāmādistadvṛddham* (A.1.1.71).
34. As an alternate the sufix - *phaK* is applied by the rule A.4.1.101.
35. The rule *oraÑ* (A.4.3.139) is an exception to the rule that prescribes - *aṆ* in a general manner. The present rule again prescribes the suffix - *aṆ* for *kopadhā* words.
36. The rule *janapada°* (A.4.2.124) is an exception to the rule that prescribes- *aṆ* in a general manner. The present rule again enjoins- *aṆ*.

37. See Note 27.
38. See Section 2.4.
39. *A*.6.1.165.
40. *A*.6.1.164.
41. *A*.6.1.197.
42. *A*.6.1.185.
43. *A*.6.1.197.
44. *A*.3.1.4.
45. *A*.6.1.217.
46. *A*.6.1.193.

CHAPTER - III
MORPHOLOGICAL FEATURES INVOLVED IN TADDHITA-FORMATION

A. MORPHOLOGICAL ANALYSIS OF THE TADDHITA-SUFFIXES

3.0. *Introduction*

Word-Formation or the process of deriving new forms of words from the existing ones by the addition of suffixes involves reference to a base which may either be a word or a stem or a root. While the word could function independently, a stem or a root and also a suffix cannot be so. The TFRs, like other WFRs, have a wide range of suffixes to be added to varied types of bases. The present chapter is devoted to a study of the various suffixes and the bases in regard to TF. In other words, this chapter deals with a morphological study of the TFRs.

3.0.1. A Unique feature that pertains to TS is that one and the same suffix is prescribed to signify a variety of meanings while certain suffixes are enjoined to convey an identical sense. Of these, the former set of suffixes falls under the morphological domain, while the latter, under the semantic domain.

To begin with, we shall discuss the suffixes that fall under the morphological domain which is known as *pratyayādhikāra*.

3.1. *Taddhita-Suffixes that fall under Morphological Domain*

There are six major types of suffixes that come under Morphological domain (*pratyayādhikāra*).[1]

Section - [A.4.1.76-5.4.160]

Taddhita [A.4.1.75]

- I - aṆ A.4.1.83 4.3.168
- II - ṭhaK 4.4.1-74
- III - yaT 4.4.75 4.4.144
- IV - cha 5.1.1-17
- V - ṭhañ 5.1.18-114
- VI
  - i. Miscellaneous 5.1.115-5.3.69
  - ii. -*Ka* 5.3:70-96
  - iii. Miscellaneous 5.3.97-5.4.160

Each of the above suffixes is superseded by specific suffixes under three conditions, Phonological, Lexical and Semantics. Of these *lexical condition* comes under the domain of morphological treatment. The other two, namely, the phonological and the semantic condition come under the domain of Phonological and Semantic treatment respectively. For example, the suffix - *aṆ* is prescribed in a comprehensive manner, without any condition whatsoever, with a view to arrive at different senses in the aphorisms beginning with A.4.1.83 and ending with A.4.3.168. But to meet certain specific requirements Pāṇini prescribes special suffixes as exceptions to it. To be explicit: *aṆ* is prescribed with a view to arrive at the sense of one's offspring. But in order to arrive at the same sense, he prescribes as an exception the suffix - *iÑ* in the case of words which end in - *a*. And the application of - *iÑ* as an exception to *aṆ* is conditioned by the phonological aspect of the base.

In the same way, Pāṇini prescribes the suffix - *Ṇya* as an exception to - *aṆ* to arrive at the senses of 'One's offspring', etc., in the cases of specific bases such as *diti* and the like. And the ground for the condition of the suffix - *Ṇya* is governed by an individual lexeme.

Further Pāṇini prescribes the suffix - *yaṄ* as an exception to - *aṆ* to words such as *madhu, babhru* and the like provided the senses of the 'offspring' of *madhu* and *babhru* are respectively a brāhmin and one who comes in the line of *kauśika*. This prescription is conditioned by the *semantic aspect*.

Similar method is noticed to be applicable in the cases of other four kinds of succeeding suffixes in the above column and this will be dealt with in the sequel.

3.1.1. - *aṆ* (*A*.4.1.83-4.3.168)

The suffix - *aṆ* is prescribed in *A*.4.1.83. Its range of application extends upto *A*.4.3.168. In this section consisting of the aphorisms beginning with *A*.4.1.83 and ending with 4.3.168, 75 suffixes are enjoined as exceptions to - *aṆ* to convey specific varied senses. Among these 75 suffixes, there are four suffixes, namely, -*Ṇya*, -*aÑ*, -*naÑ* and *snaÑ* which convey all the senses that are conveyed by the suffix - *aṆ* and they are, however, conditioned by the specific lexeme. The above suffixes which are mentioned in the section that prescribes the suffix -*aṆ*; are not specified with a view to convey any specific meaning. Hence, these suffixes are applied to the stems to convey the meanings that would be conveyed by -*aṆ*. This is based upon the authority of the commentaries on the *Aṣṭādhyāyī*.[2]

The aphorism *A*.4.1.83 prescribes -*aṆ* in a general manner. The succeeding aphorisms upto *A*.4.3.168 may broadly be classified into four groups as follows:[3]

(a) the rules *A*.4.1.84 - 4.1.87;
(b) the rules *A*.4.1.92 - 4.2.91;
(c) the rules *A*.4.2.93 - 4.3.24; and
(d) the rules *A*.4.3.25 - 4.3.168

(a) *A*.4.1.84 - 4.1.87

The rules under this group prescribe for specific bases some special suffixes as exceptions to -*aṆ* to convey the meanings identified in the rules from *A*.4.1.92 - 4.3.168. However, the rule *A*.4.1.87 which prescribes special suffixes for specific bases extends upto *A*.4.1.92 - 5.2.1.

(b) *A*.4.1.92 - 4.2.91

The rules under this group prescribe the suffix - *aṆ* in an unspecified manner to convey different meanings; and they are then superseded by special rules, prescribing special suffixes for specific bases or environments wherever necessary. For example, the suffix - *aṆ* is prescribed in the senses of *tasyāpatyam* (*A*.4.1.92) 'his offspring', *tadadhīte tadveda* (*A*.4.2.59) 'one who studies or knows', etc. Under these meaning headings there are some special suffixes for specific bases such as *ata iÑ* (*A*.4.1.95) *vasantādibhyaṣṭhaK* (*A*.4.2.63), etc.

(c) *A*.4.2.93 - 4.3.24

The rules under this group prescribe special suffixes for particular bases or environments to arrive at the meanings stated in the rules from *A*.4.3.25 - 4.3.133.

(d) *A*.4.3.25 - 4.3.168

The rules under this group prescribe the meanings for the suffixes stated in (a) and (c) along with the special rules prescribing special suffixes for specific bases or environments wherever necessary.

The difference between the nature and scope of the rules grouped under (a) and (c) lies in this that the rules under head (a) have a wider scope of application, that is, they are available in all the meanings stated from *A*.4.1.92 - 4.3.168. But the rules under the head (c) apply only in those cases which have been stated in the rules *A*.4.3.25 - 4.3.133. In short, the rules under (a) are applicable in regard to the meanings under group (b) and (d) both. But the rules under the group (c) are applicable in regard to the meanings under group (d) only.

We shall in the following pages discuss the rules that supersede -*aṆ* and prescribe other suffixes in relation to specific bases.

3.1.1.1. *The Suffix aṆ and its variants belonging to the Group (A) and (B)*:

In this section it is only the lexically conditioned variants that are taken up for discussion. In regard to the remaining two conditions, namely, Phonology and Semantics, phonology has already been dealt with and semantics will be treated in the sequel.

Group (**a**)

Base	***Meaning***	***Example***
1. *aṆ - Ṇya/ditya,* etc. A.4.1.85	The suffix -*aṆ* expresses all the meanings stated under its domain.	*daityaḥ*, etc.
2. *aṆ/utsa* etc. (A.4.1.86)	- do -	*autsaḥ*, etc.
3. *naÑ/snaÑ stri* and *pumān.* A.4.1.87.	These suffixes express the meanings stated upto the rules A.5.2.1, besides all the meanings expressed by - *aṆ*	*strainaḥ paumsnaḥ*

Group (b) treats the suffixes which are exceptions to - *aṆ* and which are applicable to arrive at specific senses.

Base	***Sense***	***Example***
1. *aṆ*		
a. aṆ - añ A.4.1.68 The words expressing the people of a country or a king like *Iksvaku* and others.	'his offspring'	*aikṣvākavaḥ*
b. The words *dvaipa* and *vaiyāghra.* A.4.2.12	'chariot covered with'	*dvaipaḥ*, etc.
c. *Khaṇḍika* A.4.2.45	'a group thereof'	*khāṇḍikam*

d. *saṅkala*, etc. A.4.2.75	'The meanings listed in *A*.4.2.67-70[4]	*saṅkalaḥ*
2. *iÑ*		
a. *bahu*, etc. A.4.1.96.	'one's offspring'	*bāhaviḥ*
b. *sutangama*, etc. A.4.2.80	'The meanings listed in *A*.4.2.67-70	*sautaṅgamiḥ*
3. *iNi - i*		
a. / *pāṇḍukambala* A.4.2.11	'chariot covered with'	*pāṇḍukambalī*
b. / *khala* A.4.2.51	'a group thereof'	*khalinī*
c. / *anubrāhmaṇa* A.4.2.62	'one who studies or knows'	*anubrāhmaṇī*
d. / *prekṣa*, etc. A.4.2.80	'The meanings listed in *A*.4.2.67-70	*prekṣī*
4. *ila*		
/ *kāśa*, etc. A.4.2.80	'The meanings listed in *A*.4.2.67-70	*kāśilaḥ*
5. *ka(K) - ka*		
/ *ṛṣya*, *varāha*, etc. A.4.2.80	'The meanings listed in *A*.4.2.67-70	*ṛṣyakam* *vārāhakaḥ*
6. *kaṭyaC - kaṭya*		
/ *ratha* A.4.2.51	'a group thereof'	*rathakaṭyā*
7. *ghaN - iya*		
/ *śukra* and *apoNaptṛ*, etc. A.4.2.26-27	'that which is one's divine being'	*śukriyam* *aponaptriyam*
8. *cha - Īya*		
a. / *svasṛ* and *bhrātṛ* A.4.1.143-44	'his offspring'	*svasrīyaḥ* *bhrātrīyaḥ*
b. / words belonging to *Dvandva* compound like *tiṣyapunarvasū*, etc. *A*.4.2.6.	'the time related to a specific star'	*tiṣyapunarvasavīyaḥ*

c. / *dyāvāpṛthivi*, etc. A.4.2.31	'that which is one's divine being'	*dyāvāpṛthivīyam*
d. / *keśa*, etc. A.4.2.48	'a group thereof'	*keśīyam*
e. / *sarkarā* and *utkarā*, etc. A.4.2.83 & 90	'The meanings listed in A.4.2.67-'70'	*śarkarīyam* *utkarīyaḥ*
9. *chaN* - *īya*		
a. / *pitṛsvas* and *mātṛsvasṛ* A.4.1.132 & 134	'his offspring'	*paitṛsvaśīyaḥ* *mātṛśvaśrīyaḥ*
b. / *kṛśāsva* etc. A.4.2.80	'The meanings listed in A.4.2.67-'70'	*kārśvasvīyam*
10. *Nya* - *ya*		
/ *pragāda* etc. A.4.2.80	'The meanings listed in A.4.2.67-'70'	*prāgādyaḥ*
11. *TyaN* - *ya*		
/ *soma* A.4.2.30	'that which is one's divine being'	*saumyam*
12. *ṭhaK* - *ika*		
a. / *lākṣa*, etc. A.4.2.2	'dyeing with'	*lākṣikam*
b. / *dadhi* and *udaśvit* A.4.2.18-19	'cooked therein'	*dādhikam* *audaśvikaḥ*
c. / *āgrahāyana* etc. and *phalgunī* A.4.2.22-23	'the period in which the full moon day falls'	*āgrahāyanikaḥ* *phālgunikaḥ*
d. / *vasanta* A.4.2.63	' one who studies or knows'	*vāsantikaḥ*
e. / *kumuda* etc., and the word *sarkara* A.4.2.80 & 84	' The meanings listed in A.4.2.67-'70'	*kaumudikam* *śarkarikam*
13. *ṭhaC* - *ika*		
/ *kumuda*, etc. A.4.2.80	'The meanings listed in A.4.2.67-'70'	*kumudikam*

14. *ṭhaÑ - ika*

a. / *mahārāja* etc. *A*.4.2.35	'that which is one's divine being'.	*māhārājikam*
b. / *kavacin* *A*.4.2.41	'a collection thereof'	*kāvacikam*

15.*ḌmatuP - mat*

/ *kumuda*, etc. *A*.4.2.87	'The meanings listed in *A*.4.2.67-'70'	*kumudvān*

16.*ḌvalaC - val*

/ *naḍa*, etc., *A*.4.2.88	'The meanings listed in *A*.4.2.67-'70 '	*naḍvalaḥ*

17.*ḌyaT and Ḍya - ya*

/ *vāmadeva* *A*.4.2.9	'sāman intuitively perceived by'	*vāmadevyam*

18.*ḍhaK - eya*

a. / The words ending infeminine gender *A*.4.1.120	'his offspring'	*vainateyaḥ*
b. / *kali* *A*.4.2.8	'*sāman* intuitively perceived by'	*kāleyam*
c. / *agni* *A*.4.2.33	'that which is one's divine being'	*āgneyaḥ*

19.*ḍhaÑ - eya*

a. / The words designating quadruples like *Kamaṇḍalu* and the words *gṛṣṭi*, etc. *A*.4.1.135-36	'his offspring'	*kāmaṇḍaleyaḥ* *gārṣṭeyaḥ*
b. / *kṣīra* *A*.4.2.20	'cooked therein'	*kṣaireyī*
c. / *sakhi*, etc., *A*.4.2.80	'The meanings listed in *A*.4.2.67-'70'	*sākheyaḥ*

20.*Nya - ya*		
a. / *kurū*, etc., A.4.1.151 & 172	'his offspring'	*kauravyaḥ*
b. / *saṅkāśa*, etc., A.4.2.80	'The meanings listed in A.4.2.67-'70'	*sāṅkāśyam*
21.*taL - ta*		
/ *grāma*, etc., A.4.2.43	' a group thereof'	*grāmatā*
22.*tra*		
/ *go* A.4.2.51	'a group thereof'	*gotrā*
23.*phaK - āyana*		
/ *pakṣa*, etc. A.4.2.80	'The meanings listed in A.4.2.67-'70'	*pākṣāyaṇaḥ*
24.*phiÑ - āyana*		
/ *karṇa*, etc., A.4.2.80	'The meanings listed in A.4.2.67-'70'	*kārṇāyaṇaḥ*
25.*bhaktal - bhakta*		
/ *aiṣukāri*, etc. A.4.2.54	'a region inhabited by them'	*aiṣukāri bhaktam*
26.*matuP - mat*		
/ The words designating the names of a river like *udumbara*, etc., and also the words *madhu* etc. A.4.2.82	'The meanings listed in A.4.2.67-'70'	*udumbarāvati madhumān*
27.*ya*		
a. / The words *pāśa*, etc., and also the word *khala*. A.4.2.50	'a collection thereof'	*pāśya khalya*
b. / *bala*, etc. A.4.2.80	'The meanings listed in A.4.2.67-'70'	*balyam*

28. *yaÑ - ya*		
/ The words belonging to the *kedāra* group and the words *keśa*, etc. A.4.2.40, 48	'a collection thereof'	*kaidaryam* *kaiśyam*
29. *yaT - ya*		
a. / *śūla*, etc., A.4.2.17	'cooked therein'	*śūlyam*
b. /The words belonging to the *Vāyu* group and also.the words *dyāvapṛthivī* etc A.4.2.32	'that which is one's divine being'	*vāyavyam* *dyāvāpṛthivyam*
30. *yaN - ya*		
/ *brāhmaṇa*, etc. A.4.2.42	' a group thereof'	*brāhmaṇyam*
31. *vidhaL - vidha*		
/ *bhauriki*, etc. A.4.2.54	' a region inhabited'	*bhaurikividham*
32. *VuÑ - aka*		
a. /*gotra*, *kedāra*, etc. A.4.2.39-40	'a collection thereof'	*gloucukāya-nakam* *kaidāryakam*
b. / *rājanya*, etc. A.4.2.53	'a region inhabited'	*rājanyakaḥ*
c. /*arīhana*, etc. A.4.2.80	'The meanings listed in A.4.2.67-'70'	*ārīhanakam*
33. *VuN - aka*		
/ *krama*, etc., A.4.2.61	'One who studies or knows'	*kramakaḥ*
34. *sa*		
/ *tṛṇa*, etc. A.4.2.80	'The meanings listed in A.4.2.67-'70'	*tṛṇasam*

3.1.1.2. *Rules in the śaiṣika section* (A.4.2.92 - 4.3.133) *belonging to group (c) and (d)* :

The rules from A.4.2.92 (*śeṣe*) upto A.4.3.24 prescribe special suffixes for specific bases or environments to convey the meanings stated in the rules that fall in between A.4.3.25 to 4.3.133. These meaning-rules are actually referred to by the word *śeṣa.*[5] These rules (A.4.3.25 - 4.3.133) include the general ones that prescribe the suffixes *aṆ*, *gha*, etc. that are to be applied to specific bases to convey the senses listed in the rules referred to above. There are nearly 25 meanings which are conveyed by the addition of the *śaiṣika*-suffixes.

As explained above, the rules under the group (c) and (d) belong to the domain of *śaiṣika* excepting the rules that lie in between A.4.3.133-168. The rules under (c), namely, A.4.2.92 to 4.3.24 are different from that of (d), namely, A.4.3.25 to 4.3.168 in some respect. As it has already been stated that in the rules of group (c) excluding A.4.2.92 we find some special suffixes and bases as exceptions to the general suffixes *aṆ*. These suffixes are actually applied to all the meanings stated in the rules from 4.3.25 to 4.3.133. But in the case of the rules that belong to group (d) we find special suffixes to be applied to certain bases. And, these special suffixes supersede the general suffix - *aÑ* in specific instances. To be explicit, a special suffix is prescribed with reference to a base to arrive at a specific meaning. It cannot be applied to any other base to convey a different sense. In this way, the special suffix supersedes the suffix - *aṆ*.

In the sections other than the *śaiṣika*, Pāṇini first specifies certain suffixes along with the intended meanings to be arrived at by their addition. Then he sets forth the rules that prescribe certain suffixes that supersede the earlier ones. But in the *śaiṣika* section, he first specifies the suffixes to be added to select bases. Then he gives a separate list of the meanings that are intended to be arrived at by the addition of these suffixes.

1.	*A*.4.3.25	'born there'
2.	*A*.4.3.38	'made, gained, bought', etc.
3.	*A*.4.3.39	'generally or abundantly found'
4.	*A*.4.3.41	'possibility'
5.	*A*.4.3.43	'proper, flowering, ripening'
6.	*A*.4.3.44	'sown'
7.	*A*.4.3.47	'to be repaid as a debt'
8.	*A*.4.3.51	'a prowling wild beast'
9.	*A*.4.3.52	'this is his habit, custom'
10.	*A*.4.3.53	'being or obtaining there'
11.	*A*.4.3.66	'a commentary of a text'
12.	*A*.4.3.74	'arrived at from a particular place'
13.	*A*.4.3.83	'first appearance'
14.	*A*.4.3.85	'that which leads to a particular destination or one who proceeds towards a particular destination'.
15.	*A*.4.3.86	'that which is a threshold to a city'
16.	*A*.4.3.82	'a work composed relating to a particular theme'
17.	*A*.4.3.89	'dwelling place'
18.	*A*.4.3.90	'ancestral residence'
19.	*A*.4.3.95	'that which is the object of devotion'
20.	*A*.4.3.101	'propagated by him'
21.	*A*.4.3.112	'having the same direction with that'
22.	*A*.4.3.115	'that which is initiated by one'
23.	*A*.4.3.116	'a text that has been composed by one'
24.	*A*.4.3.120	'that which belongs to one'

The general suffix - *aṆ* along with its exceptions, that is, *A*.4.1.84-87 has occurred in all the above meanings. Apart from these, the special suffixes for specific bases or environments which are also exceptions to the general suffix - *aṆ* will be described in the following sections. Let us first begin with the discussion on the suffixes that fall under the group (C) (*A*.4.2.92 - 4.3.24).

The following 18 suffixes are added to bases to arrive at the meanings listed in *A*.4.3.24 to 120.

Group (C)

1. - *aÑ*		
A.4.2.106-7	The word ending in *tīra* and the words belonging to *madra* group having *dik* as the first word.	*kākatīram* *paurvamadraḥ*, etc.
2. *khaÑ* - *ina*		
A.4.2.93 and 4.3.1	The words *avār-apāra, grāma, yuṣmad* and *asmad.*	*avārapārīṇaḥ* *grāmīṇaḥ* *yauṣmākīnaḥ* *āsmākīnaḥ*
3. *gha* - *iya*		
A.4.2.93	*rāṣṭra*, etc.	*rāṣṭriyaḥ*
4. *cha* - *īya*		
A.4.2.137	The bases having the word *garta* at its end.	*vṛkagartīyam*
5. - *Ña*		
A.4.2.107	The bases which have as their initial word the one that conveys the sense of direction.	*paurvaśālaḥ*
6. - *Ñiṭha* - *ika*		
A.4.2.116	The bases belonging to the *kāśi* group.	*kāśika*
7. - *Ñya* - *ya*		
A.4.2.106	The bases which have at their end the words that convey the sense of colour.	*śaivarūpyam*

8. - *Ṭyu (L) - ana*		
A.4.2.105	The words *aiṣama*, etc.,	*aiṣamastanam*
4.3.23	and also *sāyam*, etc.	*sāyantanam*
9. - *ṭhaK - ika*		
A.4.2.102	the word *kantha*	*kānthikaḥ*
10.- *ṭhaÑ - ika*		
a. *A*.4.2.116	The words belonging to *kāśī* group.	*kāśikā*
b. *A*.4.3.6	The base *ardha* which has as its initial word the one that signifies direction.	*paurvārdhikam*
c. *A*.4.3.11	The word denoting time (*kāla*)	*māsikam*
11.- *ḍhaK - eya*		
A.4.2.97	The words belonging to the *nakṣatra* group.	*nādeyam*
12.- *dhakaÑ*		
A.4.2.95	The words belonging to the *kartrī* group	*kārtreyakaḥ*
13.-*tyaK - tya*		
A.4.2.98	The words *dakṣiṇā*, etc.	*dākṣiṇātyaḥ*
14.- *tyaP - tya*		
A.4.2.104-5	The indeclinable words *yatra*, *aisama*, etc.	*yatratyaḥ* *aiṣamatyam*
15.- *ma*		
A.4.3.8	The word *madhya*	*madhyamaḥ*
16.- *yaT - ya*		
a. *A*.4.2.101	The words *div*, etc.	*divyam*
b. *A*.4.3.4	The word *ardha*	*ardhyam*
c. *A*.4.3.6	The word *ardha* having as its initial word the one that conveys the sense of direction.	*pūrvārdhyam*

17.*vuÑ - aka*

A.4.2.127	The words belonging to the *dhūma* group.	*dhaumakaḥ*

18.*Sphak - āyana*

A.4.2.99	The word *kāpiśya*	*kāpiśyāyanam*

3.1.1.3. *Group (D)*:

	Base	***Meaning***	***Example***
1.- *KaN - ka*			
A.4.3.32	The words *sindhu*	'born'	*sindhukaḥ*
2.-*Cha - īya*			
A.4.3.63-64	The words *jihvā-mūla* etc., and also the words ending with *varga*	'being or obtaining therein'	*jihvāmūlīyaḥ kavargīyam*
b.*A*.4.3.88	The words *śiśukranda*	' the work composed relating to a particular theme'	*śiśukran-dīyaḥ*
3.- *chaṆ - īya*			
A.4.3.94	The word *śalātura*	'dwelling place'	*śālāturiyaḥ*
4.- *Ñya - ya*			
a.*A*.4.3.58-59	The word *gambhīra*, and the words belonging to *avyayībhāva* compound	'found or obtained therein'	*gāmbhīryam pārimukhyam*

b.*A*.4.3.84	The word *vidūra*	'first appearance'	*vaidūryaḥ*
c.*A*.4.3.92	The words belonging to *śaṇḍika* group	'dwelling place'	*śāṇḍikyaḥ*
d.*A*.4.3.128	The word *chandoga*, etc.	'that which belongs to one'	*chāndogyam*
5.- *thaK* - *ika*			
a.*A*.4.3.40	The words *upajānu*, etc.	'generally found there in'	*aupajānukaḥ*
b.*A*.4.2.124	The words *hala* and *śīra*	'that which belongs to one'	*hālikam* *śairikam*
6.- *ṭhaÑ* - *ika*			
a. *A*.4.3.60	The words consisting of an *avyayībhāva* compound with *antar* as a prior member.	'being or obtaining therein'	*āntarveśmikam*
b.*A*.4.3.61	The words consisting of an *avyayībhāva* compound ending in *grāma* co-occurring with preverbs *pari* and *anu*	'being or obtaining therein'	*pārigrāmikaḥ*
c.*A*.4.3.97	The word *mahārāja*	'that which is the object of devotion'	*māharājikaḥ*
7.-*ḍhaK* - *eya*			
A.4.3.94	The word *tudi*, etc.	'dwelling place'	*taudeyaḥ*

8.-*ḍhaÑ* - *eya*			
a.*A*.4.3.42	The word *krośa*	'fit, suitable, adequate'	*kauśeyam*
b.*A*.4.3.58	The words *dṛti*, etc.	'found or obtained therein'	*dārteyam*
c.*A*.4.3.94	The word *varmatī*	'dwelling place'	*vārmateyaḥ*
9.- *Ṇini* - *ini*			
A.4.3.103	The words *kaśyapa*, etc.	'(it is) propagated by him'	*kāśyapī*
10.- *tasI* - *tas*			
A.4.3.114	The word *uras*	'having the same direction with that'	*urastaḥ*
11.*mayaṬ* - *maya*			
A.4.3.82	The words designating a cause or human being	'arrived at from a particular source'	*samamayam devadatta-mayam*
12.- *yaK* - *ya*			
A.4.3.94	The word *kūcavāra*	'ancestral residence'	*kaucavāryaḥ*
13. a.*A*.4.3.54-55	The words *dik*, etc., and also the words designating a member of the body	'being or obtaining therein'	*diśyam dantyam*
b.*A*.4.3.114	The word *uras*	'having the same direction with that'	*urasyaḥ*

14.- *vuÑ - aka*			
a.*A*.4.3.77	The words designating a person related either through learning or through blood	'arrived at from a particular source'	*aupadhyāyakaḥ* *paitāmahakaḥ*
b.*A*.4.3.99	The words representing patronymics or warriors	'that which is an object of devotion'	*aupagavakaḥ* *nākulakaḥ*
c.*A*.4.3.126	The words designating patronymics and those representing Vedic schools	'that which belongs to it'	*aupagavakam* *kāṭhakam*
15.*vuN - aka*			
a.*A*.4.3.28	The words *pūrvāhna*, etc.	'born in that time'	*pūrvāhnakaḥ*
b.*A*.4.3.48	The words *kalāpin*, etc.	'to be repaid as a debt'	*kalāpakam*
c.*A*.4.3.98	The words *vāsudeva* and *arjuna*	'that which is the object of devotion'	*vāsudevakaḥ* *arjunakaḥ*
16.- *rūpya*			
A.4.3.81	The words designating a cause or a human being	'originating that'	*samarupyam* *devadattarupyam*
17.- *ṢṭhaN - ika*			
	The words *paurodāśa* and *purodāśa*	'a commentary thereon'	*paurodaśikaḥ* *purodaśikaḥ*

3.1.1.4. The following suffixes are exceptions to the general suffix - *aṆ* convey the sense of that which is transformation or modification of a particular thing and also the sense of the parts of animals, herbs and trees.

1.- *aÑ*

a.*A*.4.3.54	The words designating animals and the class of words beginning with *rajata*	*śaukam rājatam*
b.*A*.4.3.168	The word *paraśu*,[6] etc.	*pāraśavam*

2.- *mayaṬ* - *maya*

A.4.3.146	The word *piṣṭa*	*piṣṭamayam*

3.- *yaÑ* - *ya*[7]

A.4.3.168	The word *kaṁsa*	*kaṁsya*

4.- *VuÑ* - *aka*

A.4.3.158	The words *uṣṭra, umā* and *ūrṇā*	*auṣṭrakaḥ aumakaḥ aurṇakaḥ*

3.1.2.0. - *ṭhaK* - *ika (A.4.4.1) prāgvateṣṭhaK*

- *thaK* - *ika,* is one of the general suffixes that have been treated by Pāṇini in a more or less similar manner. The rule *A*.4.4.1, wherein - *thaK* has been laid down as a general TS is in the same fashion as that of *A*.4.1.83. Like other general TS, here too, the word *prāk* 'before' in the rule *A*.4.4.1 has been incorporated to explain the nature of the *adhikāra* of this rule. Just as-*aṆ* the general suffix - *thaK* also has some exceptions in so far as some specific stems or environments are concerned.

3.1.2.1 The following are exceptions to the general suffix - *thaK* - *ika* for specific bases.

	Base	***Meaning***	***Example***
1. - *aṆ*			
a. *A*.4.4.4	The word *kulattha*	'seasoned'	*kaulattham*
b. *A*.4.4.18	The word *kuṭilika*	'carries or bears with it'	*kauṭilikaḥ*
c. *A*.4.4.25	The word *mudga*	'mixed with'	*maudgaḥ*
d. *A*.4.4.48	The words *mahiṣa,* etc.	'that which is fit to be pursued'	*māhiṣam*

e. *A*.4.4.56	The words *maḍḍuka*, etc.	'proficiency or dexterity in carrying out one's activity'	*māḍḍukaḥ*
f. *A*.4.4.68	The word *bhakta*	'the one to whom cook-ed food is regularly offered'	*bhāktaḥ*
2. *inī - in*			
A.4.4.23	*cūrṇa*	'mixed with it'	*cūrṇinaḥ*
3. *īkaK - ika*			
A.4.4.59	The word *śakti* etc..	'that which is one's weapon'	*śāktīkaḥ*
4. *kaK(N) - ka*			
A.4.4.21	The words *apamitya*, etc.	'originated or accom-plished in'	*apamitya-kam* *āpamitya-kam*
5. *cha - īya*			
A.4.4.14	The word *āyudha*	'that which is one's means of livelihood'	*āyudhīyaḥ*
6. *TithaN - ika*			
A.4.4.67	The words *śrāṇa*, etc.	'allotted to him right-fully'	*śrāṇikaḥ*
7. *thaÑ - ika*			
a. *A*.4.4.6	*gopuccha*	'crosses with it'	*gaupu-cchikaḥ*
b. *A*.4.4.11	*svagaṇa*	'one who goes on by means there-of'	*svāgaṇikaḥ*

c. *A*.4.4.13	The words *vasna*, etc.	'earns his livelihood with it'	*vāsnikaḥ*
d. *A*.4.4.38	*ākranda*	'runs'	*ākrandikaḥ*
e. *A*.4.4.52	*lavaṇa*	'one's commodity is for sale'	*lāvaṇikaḥ*
f. *A*.4.4.58	*paraśvadha*	'that which is one's weapon'	*pāraśvadhi-kaḥ*
8. *ṭhaN - ika*			
a. *A*.4.4.7	The words *nau*, etc.	'crosses with it'	*nāvikaḥ*
b. *A*.4.4.42	*pratipatham*	'one who goes along the road'	*prātipathi-kaḥ*
c. *A*.4.4.70	*agāra* as a final member in a word	'appointed or employed therein'	*aevāgārikaḥ*
9. - *Ṇa - a*			
A.4.4.62	The words *chatra*, etc.	'one's habit or nature'	*chātraḥ*
10.- *Ṇya - ya*			
A.4.4.44	'*pariṣad*'	'one who associates oneself'	*pāriṣadyaḥ*
11.- *maP - ma*			
A.4.4.20	The words ending in *ktri*	'originated or accom-plished by it'	*paktrimam*
12.- *ṢṭhaC - ika*			
A.4.4.31	The words *kusīdaka*, etc.	'gives some-thing with detestable attitude'	*kusīdikī*

13.- *ṢṭhaN - ika*

a. *A.*4.4.10	The words *parpa,* etc.	'one who goes on by means thereof'	*parpikī*
b. *A.*4.4.16	The words *bhastra,* etc.	'carries or bears'	*bhastrikī*
c. *A.*4.4.31	The words *kusīdaka,* etc.	'gives something with detestable attitude'	*kusīdikī*
a. *A.*4.4.53	The words *kisara,* etc.	'one's commodity is for sale'	*kisarikaḥ*

14.- *ṢṭhaL-ika*

*A.*4.4.9	*ākarṣa*	'crosses with it'	*ākarṣikaḥ*

3.1.3.0 - *yaT* - *ya prāgghitādyaT* [*A.*4.4.75-144]

Like other *adhikāra* rules which lay down different general suffixes in the *Taddhita*-section, the above rule too prescribes a general suffix. The latter too has exceptions in so far as specific bases or environments are concerned. The force of the above rule must normally extends upto the aphorism - *tasmaihitam* (A.5.1.5) wherein the word *hitam* occurs. But since the aphorism - *prākkrītācchaḥ* (*A.*5.1.1) prescribes another suffix, we have to take the aphorism *A.*4.4.75 as extending upto *A.*4.4.144 only.

3.1.3.1. We shall now set forth the exceptions to the suffix - *yaT.*

	Base	Meaning	Example
1.- *aṆ*			
a.*A.*4.4.80	*śakaṭa*	'that which draws'	*śākaṭaḥ*
b.*A.*4.4.94	*uras*	'created out of desire'	*aurasaḥ*
c.*A.*4.4.112	*veśanta*	'occurring therein'	*vaiśantī*

d.*A*.4.4.126	*aśvimān*[8]	'setting up sacrifical bricks'	*āśvinī*
2.-*kha-ina*			
A.4.4.78	*sarvadhura*	'that which draws'	*sarvadhurī-naḥ*
3.-*khaÑ-īna*			
A.4.4.99	'*pratijana*, etc.	'one who is good at or proficient in something'	*prātijanīnaḥ*
4.-*gha-iya*			
a.*A*.4.4.117	*agra*	'occurring therein'	*agriyaḥ*
b.*A*.4.4.118	The words *samudra*, etc.	'occurring therein'	*samudriyaḥ*
5.-*ghaN-iya*			
A.4.4.115	*tugra*	'occurring therein'	*tugriyaḥ*
6.- *cha* - *īya*			
A.4.4.117	*agra*	'occurring therein'	*agrīyaḥ*
7.- *Na* - *a*			
A.4.4.129	*madhu*	'in the sense of possession'	*mādhavaḥ*
8.-*thaK-ika*			
a.*A*.4.4.81	*hala*, etc.	'that which draws'	*hālikaḥ*
b.*A*.4.4.102	The words *katha*, etc.	'one who is good at something'	*kāthikaḥ*
9.-*thaÑ-ika*			
A.4.4.103	The words *guḍa*, etc.	'one who is good at something'	*gauḍikaḥ*
10.-*Dya(T)-ya*			
A.4.4.113	The words *śrotas*, etc.	'occurring therein'	*śrotyaḥ*
11.- *ḌyaṆ-ya*			
A.4.4.111	The words *pathi*, etc.	'occurring therein'	*pāthyaḥ*
12.-*ḍha-eya*			
A.4.4.106	*sabhā* in Vedic language	'one who is good at something'	*sabheyaḥ*

13.- *ḍhaK-eya*			
A.4.4.77	*dhura*	'that which draws'	*dhaureyaḥ*
14.- *ḍhaÑ - eya*			
A.4.4.104	*pathi*	'one who is good at something'	*pātheyam*
15.- *Ṇa - a*			
a.A.4.4.85	*anna*	'one who obtains'	*ānnaḥ*
b.A.4.4.120	*bhakta*	'one who is good at something'	*bhāktaḥ*
16.- *Ṇya - ya*			
A.4.4.101	*pariṣada*	'one who is good at something'	*pāriṣadyaḥ*
17.- *matuP*			
A.4.4.127	*mūrdhan*	'setting up of sacrificial bricks'	*mūrdhanvatī* *mūrdhanvān*
18.- *ya*			
A.4.4.105	*sabhā*	'one who is good at something'	*sabhyaḥ*
19.- *yaN - ya*			
A.4.4.114	The words *sagarbha*, etc.	'occurring therein'	*sagarbhyaḥ*
20.- *yaL - ya*			
A.4.4.31	The word *bhaga* which is having the words *veśa*, etc., in its initial position	'in the sense of possession'	*veśobhagyaḥ*

3.1.4. *Cha - īya prākkrītācchaḥ* (A.5.1.1 - 5.1.18)

cha is a general suffix. Like other TS, this too has exceptions, and we shall now deal with the latter.

	Base	Meaning	Example
1.- *kha* - *īna*			
A.5.1.9	The words *ātman,* etc.	'that which is beneficial'	*ātmanīnam*
2.*khaÑ* - *īna*			
A.5.1.11	The words *māṇava,* etc.	'that which is beneficial'	*māṇavīnam*
3.*Ñya* - *ya*			
A.5.1.14	The words *ṛṣabha,* etc.	'to convey the sense of something which is nursed with the idea of helping it to grow into the form of some other thing.	*ārṣabhyaḥ*
4.- *ḍhaÑ* - *eya*			
A.5.1.10	The words *sarva,* etc.	'that which is beneficial'	*sarvīyam*
5.- *Ṇa* - *a*			
A.5.1.10	The words *sarva,* etc.	- do -	*sārvam*
6.- *thyaN* - *thya*			
A.5.1.8	The words *aja,* etc.	- do -	*ajathyā*
7.*yaT* - *ya*			
a.*A*.5.1.2	The words ending in the vowel *u* and the words *go,* etc.[9]	- do -	*saṅkavyam* *gavyam*
b.*A*.5.1.4	The words *haviṣ,* etc.	- do -	*haviṣyam*
c.*A*.5.1.7	The words *khala,* etc.	- do -	*khalyam*

3.1.5.0 - *thaÑ* - *ika prāgvateṣṭhaÑ* (*A*.5.1.18-114)

In these aphorisms wherein the meanings alone are specified and not the suffixes therein the suffix - *ṭhaÑ* is to be used in respect of the meanings so specified. This suffix - *ṭhaÑ* is referred to in the aphorism *A*.5.1.18 and its range of application extends upto *A*.5.1.115. In the aphorism *A*.5.1.19, however, the suffix - *ṭhaK* is enjoined to convey those meanings which are intended to be conveyed by the addition of the suffix - *ṭhaÑ* to bases. But this -*ṭhaK*, although it conveys the same senses as those of - *ṭhaÑ* is to be added to specific base. In other words, - *ṭhaÑ* is enjoined exclusively with reference to certain bases. It is in this sense, the suffix - *ṭhaK* is to be considered as an exception to - *ṭhaÑ* although it fully comes under the domain of - *ṭhaÑ*. The range of application of the suffix - *ṭhaK* extends upto *A*.5.1.63.

The aphorisms that fall under the domain of the suffix - *ṭhaK* begin with *A*.5.1.19 and end with *A*.5.1.63. Herein too there are suffixes — twelve in number which are prescribed as exceptions to - *ṭhaK*.

Out of these twelve suffixes, certain suffixes are mentioned first in the aphorisms. Then only their meanings are specified. Certain other suffixes are mentioned in the aphorisms along with their meanings. It must be added here that the meanings that are to be conveyed by - *ṭhaK* are those that are to be conveyed by - *ṭkaÑ* only. There is only the difference in the bases to which - *ṭhaK* is to be added.

The difference between these two kinds of suffixes lies in this that the first group of suffixes is to be applied to all the meanings mentioned upto the rule *A*.5.1.63, whereas the latter group of suffixes specified along with the meanings in the aphorisms is to be applied only to arrive at those specific meanings.

The - *ṭhaÑ* - *adhikara* may be classified as follows:

a. *A*.5.1.18 - 5.1.114
b. *A*.5.1.19 - 5.1.63
c. *A*.5.1.18 - 5.1.36
d. *A*.5.1.37 - 5.1.514

(a) *A*.5.1.18 - 5.1.114

Under this group the general suffix - *ṭhaÑ* covers all the meanings mentioned upto the rule *A*.5.1.114. As in the case of other general suffixes here too there are some special suffixes enjoined as exceptions in regard to specific stems or environments.

(b) *A*.5.1.19 - 5.1.63

Under this group the suffix - *ṭhaK* is enjoined. This is an exception to the general suffix - *ṭhaÑ* and it covers all the meanings mentioned upto the rule *A*.5.1.63. The aphorisms wherein - *ṭhaK* is enjoined form part of the rules that prescribe the suffix - *ṭhaÑ*.

(c) *A*.5.1.18 - 5.1.36

This group consists of nearly eleven suffixes. As in the *śaiṣika* section, here too the above suffixes can broadly be applied to arrive at the meanings listed in the rules upto *A*.5.1.63. The general suffix is - *ṭhaÑ*. But in regard to specific stems or environments, it is superseded by special suffixes.

(d) *A*.5.1.37 - 5.1.114

Under this group there are some special suffixes prescribed with reference to specific stems or environments along with the meaning-stating rules. These will be applied only with reference to those particular meanings. These also serve as exceptions to the general suffix - *ṭhaÑ*.

The following are the meanings stated in the rules *A*.5.1.37-63. The suffixes that the specified in the rules *A*.5.1.18-36 [including the general suffix - *ṭhaÑ*] can be applied with reference to these senses.

1. 'bought / purchased with - *A*.5.1.37;
2. 'the ground (*nimittam*) being a connection [*saṁyoga*] or ill or good omen - *utpātau A*.5.1.38;
3. 'its lord or ruler' - *īśvaraḥ* - *A*.5.1.42;
4. 'known as' - *vidita iti* - *A*.5.1.43;
5. 'field where something is sown' - *tasya vāpaḥ* - *A*.5.1.45;
6. 'the one to whom interest' (*vṛddhi*), 'rent' (*āya*), profit (*lābha*), 'tax' (*śulka*) or 'bribe' (*upadā*) is given - *A*.5.1.47;
7. 'unlawful removal from one place to another (*harati*) conducting something to by means of a conveyance (*vahati*), 'bringing something from a place to the point where the agent is' - *āvahati* - *A*.5.1.50;
8. 'the measure of (an object) which does not exceed the

measure of its container', or 'the measure (of an object) which is less than the measure of its container or 'cooking' - *A*.5.1.52;

9. 'One's share' (*asyāṁśaḥ*), 'price' (*vasna*) or wage (*bhṛti*) - *A*.5.1.56;
10. 'by which something is measured' - *A*.5.1.57; and
11. 'one who is fit to receive something' - *arhati* - *A*.5.1.63.

3.1.5.1. To the general suffix - *ṭhaÑ*, the following eight suffixes are exceptions; and, they are specified in the rules *A*.5.1.18-36 with reference to specific bases to arrive at the sense listed in the rules *A*.5.1.37-63.

	Base	***Example***
1. *ṭhaÑ* - *aÑ*		
A.5.1.26	*śūrpa*	*śaurpam*
2. - *aṆ*		
a. *A*.5.1.27	The words *śatamāna*, etc.	*śātamānam*
b.	The bases having the words *dvi* and *tri* in their initial position such as *dviśāṇa*, etc.	*dvaiśāṇam*
3. - *ikaN* - *īka*		
A.5.1.33	The bases *khārī* co-occurring with the word *adhyardha* as a preceding member in a *dvigu* compound such as *adhyardhakharī*, etc.	*adhyardha-khārīkam*
4. - *kha* - *īna*		
A.5.1.24	The bases *viṁśatika* co-occurring with the word *adhyardha* as a preceding member in a *dvigu* compound such as *adhyardhaviṁśatika* etc.	*adhyardha-viṁśakīnam*

5. *ṬiṭhaN - ika*		
*A.*5.1.25	*kaṁsa*	*kaṁsikaḥ*
6. - *ṭhaK - ika*		
*A.*5.1.20	The words *niṣka*, etc., when they are not components of a compound	*naiṣkikam*
7. - *ṭhaN - ika*		
*A.*5.1.21	*śata*	*śatikam*
8. *yaT - ya*		
a. *A.*5.1.21	*śata*	*śatyam*
b. *A.*5.1.28	The bases *paṇa* co-occurring with the word *adhyardha* as a preceding member of a *dvigu* compound such as *adhyardhapaṇa*, etc.	*adhyardha-paṇyam*

3.1.5.2. To the general suffix - *ṭhaÑ*, the following suffixes serve as exceptions. These suffixes are mentioned under Group D with reference to certain bases to convey specific meanings:

	Base	Meanings	Example
1.- *ṭhaÑ - aÑ*			
a.*A.*5.1.41	The words *sarvabhūmi*, etc.	'the ground being a cause; or ill or good 'omen'	*sārva-bhaumaḥ*
b.A.5.1.61	*saptan*	'by which some-thing is measured	*sāptāni*
2.- *aṆ*			
a.*A.*5.1.41	The words *sarvabhūmi*, etc.	'the ground being a cause; or ill or good omen'	*sārva-bhaumaḥ*
b.*A.*5.1.97	The words *vyuṣṭa*, etc.	'that which is offered or accom-plished at a specific point of time'	*vaiyuṣṭam*

c.*A*.5.1.105	*rtu*	'advent of the suitable time'	*ārtavam*

3.- *ukaÑ* - *uka*

A.5.1.103	*karmaṇ*	'capability to carry out something'	*kārmukaḥ*

4.- *kaN* - *ka*

A.5.1.51	The words *vasna*, etc.	'unlawful removal from one place to another (*harati*) etc.	*vasnikaḥ*

5.- *khaÑ* - *īna*

a.*A*.5.1.53-54	The words *āḍhaka*, etc. and also the compound words of *dvigu* category	'the measure (of an object) which does not exceed the measure of its container'	*āḍhakīnaḥ*
b.*A*.5.1.85	*sama*	'directing one toward some activity by extending kindliness and courtesy to him'	*samīnaḥ*
c.*A*.5.1.82	The word *vatsara* co-occurring with the prepositions *sam* and *pari* as prior members as in *samvatsara*, etc.	'That which is accomplished during a period of time'	*saṁvat-sarīnaḥ*

6.-*khaÑ-īna*

A.5.1.71	*ṛtvik*	'one who is fit to receive something'	*ārtvijīnaḥ*

7.-*ghaN-iya*

A.5.1.68, 71	The words *pātra* and *yajña*	'one who is fit to receive it '	*pātrivaḥ* *yajñiyaḥ*

8.- *cha* - *īya*

a.*A*.5.1.40	*putra*	'the ground being a connection or ill or good omen'	*putrīyaḥ*
b.*A*.5.1.69	The words *kaḍaṅkara*, etc.	'one who is fit to receive it'	*kaḍaṅka-rīyaḥ*
c.*A*.5.1.91	The words *vatsara* occurring as a final member of compound as in *idvatsara*, etc.	'That which is accomplished during a period of time'	*idvatsa-rīyaḥ*
d.*A*.5.1.92	The words *vatsara* co-occurring with the prepositions *sam* and *pari* as prior members as in *samvatsara*, etc.	'That which is accomplished during a period of time'	*samvat–sarīyaḥ*
e.*A*.5.1.111, 112	The words *anupravacana*, etc., and also the word *samāpana* occurring with a prior member in a compound like *chandassamāpana*	'to achieve a purpose'	*anuprava–canīyam* chanda-ssama-

paniyam

9.- *ṭhaK* - *ika*

a.*A*.5.1.65	*śīrsaccheda*	'one who is fit to receive it'	*śairṣac-chedikaḥ*

10.- *ṭhaN* - *ika*

a.*A*.5.1.49	The word *bhāga*	'interest'	*bhāgikaḥ*
b.*A*.5.1.51	The words *vasna*, etc.	'unlawful removal from one place to another'	*vasnikaḥ*

11.- *Ṇa* - *a*			
a.*A*.5.1.76	*pathin*	'the activity of going invariably'	*pānthaḥ*
b.*A*.5.1.98	The words *yathā-kathā ca*, etc.	'that which is offered or accomplished at a specific point of time'	*yāthākathācam*
12.- *ṆyaT* - *ya*			
A.5.1.83	*ṣaṇmāsa*	'an object that was present throughout a period of time in the past, etc.'	*ṣaṇmāsyaḥ*
13.*yaT* - *ya*			
a.*A*.5.1.39-40	The words *go* etc., and also the word *putra*	'the ground being a connection or all or good omen'	*gavyaḥ* *putryaḥ*
b.*A*.5.1.49	*bhāga*	'one to whom interest or profit is given'	*bhāgyam*
c.*A*.5.1.65-69	The word *sīrṣaccheda* and the words *kaḍaṅkara*, etc., and also the words that are listed in *daṇḍa* and *pātra* group	'one who is fit to receive it'	*śīrṣacchedyaḥ* *kaḍaṅkaryaḥ*, *daṇḍyaḥ* *pātryaḥ*
d.*A*.5.1.100	The words *karmaṇ*, etc.	'by which one's stature is enhanced'	*karmaṇyam*
e.*A*.5.1.102	*yoga*	'one who is capable of carrying out something'	*yogyaḥ*
f.*A*.5.1.107	*kāla*	'advent of the suitable time'	*kālyaḥ*

14.- *yaP* - *ya*

A.5.1.82	The compound words of *dvigu* type like *dvi-māsa*, etc.	'an object that was present throughout the period of time in the past, etc.'	*dvimāsyaḥ*

15.- *ṢkaN* - *ka*

A.5.1.75	*pathin*	'the activity of going invariably'	*pathikaḥ*

16.- *ṢṭhaN* - *ika*

a.*A*.5.1.46	The word *pātra*.	'a field where something is sown'	*pātrikaḥ*
b.*A*.5.1.54	The word *āḍhaka* consisting of a *dvigu* compound like *dvyāḍhaka*	'which does not exceed the measure of its container'	*dvyā-ḍhakikaḥ*

3.1.6. *Miscellaneous*

The group of suffixes prescribed in the aphorisms beginning with *A*.5.1.115 to *A*.5.4.160 is markedly different from the group of TS prescribed in other aphorisms. It is thus: the former group is a collection of suffixes that are both *asvārthika* - and *svārthika*-types, while the latter one are only of *asvārthika* type. This is the reason why the former group of suffixes is designated as miscellaneous ones and is taken up for discussion separately.

Miscellaneous suffixes that fall under the categories of *asvārthika* and *svārthika* may be indicated as follows:

Suffixes* in the *Aphorisms	***asvārthika***	***svārthika***
1. *A*.5.1.115-5.2.140	- do -	———
2. *A*.5.3.1-5.4.160	———	- do -

It must be noted here that the aphorism *A*.5.3.70 enjoins the suffix *-ka* in a general manner, and the area of its operation extends upto *A*.5.3.93. Further the suffixes mentioned in the aphorisms *A*.5.4.67 to 5.4.160 are enjoined with reference to bases that are compound-words widely known as *samasanta*-suffixes.

3.2. *Bases of the Taddhita-Suffixes*

3.2.0. In the first chapter of the present work, we have discussed different types of suffixations relating to the different types of bases to which the suffixes are added. It has further been shown that the TSs are generally added to a nominal word. The rule *Ṅyāpprātipadikāt* (*A*.4.1.1) generally specifies the base for case-endings as well as the TS. And the base is either a *prātipadika* [a nominal-stem] or a stem with a feminine suffix added to it.[10] The designation *prātipadika* applies to a meaningful unit which is different from a verbal root, a suffix and a word ending with a suffix that is neither a *kṛt* nor a *taddhita*. It also applies to compound words.[11]

The operation of the aphorism *A*.4.1.1. extends upto *A*.5.4.160. Thus the range of the operation of this aphorism is vast, and it is known as *prātipadikādhikāra.*

3.2.1. Under the *prātipadikādhikāra* we find an aphorism *samarthānām prathāmad vā* (*A*.4.1.82) which enjoins the TS-s optionally. The word *samartha* in this aphorism signifies a modified base, that is, a nominal word derived by the addition of case-endings. This shows that the base with regard to the TS-s is different from the one which is referred to in the rule *A*.4.1.1. Thus the word *samartha* in *A*.4.1.82 makes one assume that in TF the base will be a nominal word. It is because the word *samartha* in the earlier rule, namely, *samarthaḥ padavidhiḥ* (*A*.2.1.1) puts a semantic condition for word-formation (*padavidhi*). This semantic condition is essential for TF too and it is known from this rule (*A*.2.1.1) itself. In the domain of the *Taddhita* also, we have the word *samartha* (*A*.4.1.82). Here this word must be taken in a sense other than the previous one. Otherwise, it would be a needless repetition. The word *samartha* in *A*.4.1.82, therefore, is taken in the sense of the modified unit that would serve as a base for the TS-s. As observed by Joshi

D.M., "The specification of the base for the *taddhita* affixes given by 4.1.1 is modified 4.1.82. This modification holds in the domain of 4.1.82, which is upto 5.2.140... According to the modification the base is to be an item specified by 4.1.1 which has already undergone an operation providing a case-marker. Such a modified base is called *pada* by 1.4.14".[12] From the above it follows that the base is modified on the basis of the underlying sentence (*vigrahavākya*) from which the *Taddhita* words are derived.

It must be added here that the modified base is a word; and a word does not serve as the base for the application of all the TS. Even stems too serve as bases. In order to identify the instances where words or stems serve as the base for the TS, it is essential to discuss the nature of two types of suffixes known as *asvārthika* and *svārthika*. The chief distinction between the *asvārthika* and the *svārthika* type of suffixes is as follows: the *asvārthika* type of suffixes are invariably applied to nominal-words, while the *svārthika* type of suffixes, to stems too.

It is thus: the *asvārthika* type of suffixes are spread over in the aphorisms beginning with *A*.4.1.82 to *A*.5.2.140. They are applied to a word which forms part of a sentence. For example, the word *dāśarathiḥ* which is derived by the addition of the suffix *iÑ* to the word *daśaratha (sya)* which forms part of the sentence *daśarathasya apatyam.* This sentence serves as the substratal base for the derived word - *dāśarathiḥ*.

The *svārthika*-type of suffixes, on the other hand, is added to a stem too. It is because the base to which it is added does not form part of a sentence. The result of this argument is that the words derived by the addition of the *svārthika*-type of suffixes do not have for their substratal base a sentence.

3.2.2. The view that the TS-s are added to words may be confirmed by making a reference to an aphorism of Pāṇini. The aphorism - *atiśāyane tamabiṣṭanau* (*A*.5.3.55) prescribes the addition of TS - *tamaP* to a base. On this ground, the suffix - *tamaP* is added to the base *pūrvāhne.* The aphorism - *ghakāla°* (*A*.6.3.17), etc., enjoins the retention of the seventh case-ending of the base *pūrvāhne* in order to arrive at the optional form *pūrvāhnetame*. We have the other form *pūrvāhnatame* wherein there is the deletion of the seventh case-ending by the rule *supodhātuprātipadikayoḥ* (A.2.4.71). The prescription of the retention of the case-ending in the base presupposes the presence of the case ending in the base and a base associated with a case-ending is a word. This serves as an evidence to sustain the contention that the TS-s are added to words.

We have said that the TS of the *svārthika* type are added to stems too. This means that they are added to stems as well as words. To be explicit: *svārthika* type of suffixes includes within itself a variety of suffixes which may be termed *atyantasvārthika*-suffixes. The latter are so called because when they are added to a base and where the resultant form is arrived at, we find no change in the meaning of the resultant form. For example, the word *devatā* which is derived out of the stem *deva* by the addition of the suffix *taL*. Here the suffix does not bring in any additional sense to the resultant form. These *antyantasvārthika* suffixes are added to stems only.[13] And the other *svārthika* suffixes are applied to both words and stems.

Apart from these there are some linguistic elements, namely, pronoun, verb and adjective which also serve as base in limited case. We shall deal with these cases now.

3.3.1. *Nominal Word*

Nominal words serve as base for the TS in the majority of cases. It is thus:

$$A \rightarrow \text{N} + \text{Af}$$
$$\text{Adj}$$

For example, *dāśarathiḥ*. Here the suffix - *iÑ* is added to the word *daśaratha(sya)* and the resultant form is *dāśarathiḥ* *(dāśarathi) - daśaratha(sya) + iÑ)*

3.3.2. *Suffixes added to Pronominal Bases*

The TS prescribed under the rule A.5.3.1-5.3.26 are called *vibhakti*. The Third Quarter of Fifth Chapter of the *Aṣṭādhyāyī* is conventionally called *vibhaktipāda*[14] as it begins with the rule which has the word *vibhakti* at the beginning. Henceforward the *svārthika*-type of suffixes are enjoined. That is, the meaning of the derived word by the addition of the suffixes prescribed in this section to the specified bases, does not involve major part of the meaning of the bases. The rules *A*.5.3.1-5.3.26 deal with suffixes to be added to pronouns. The designation of these suffixes as *vibhakti* by Pāṇini is, according to Kātyāyana, purposeful. The purposes are as follows:

1. According to the rule *halantyam* (*A*.1.3.2), the final letter of a suffix is an indicatory one which is technically termed *iT*. And, according to another rule - *tasya lopaḥ* (*A*.1.3.9), the indicatory letter shall be dropped. Now, if the above position is strictly adhered to, then forms like *rāmāḥ, rāmāt, rāmāṇām*, etc., could not be derived. It is thus: there is the addition of the suffix -*Jas* to the stem *rāma*. According to the rule *halantyam* (*A*.1.3.2), the final letter, namely *S* in the suffix -*JaS* is an indicatory one; and by the rule *tasya lopaḥ* it is to be dropped. At this stage we will be having only this form - *rāma* + a (the *J* in *Ja* being an indicatory letter by the rule *cuṭū* (*A*.1.3.7) will be dropped). The resultant form would be *rāmā* and not *rāmāḥ*.

To obviate the above unwelcome position, Pāṇini has prescribed that the final letters in the letters comprising *ta* series, *S* and *M* in the case-suffixes are not indicatory ones thus precluding the possibility of their being dropped by the application of the rule *tasya lopaḥ*.

Now in the case of the addition of the suffix -*Jas* to the stem *rāma*, the final letter of the suffix is *S*; and, by the application of the rule *na vibhaktau tusmāḥ* (*A*.1.3.3) it will not acquire the designation *iT* and so it will not be dropped. We will thus be having the form:

rāma + (J) as
Ø
rāma + *as*
rāmās - *rāmāḥ*

In order to arrive at the desired forms such as *idānīm* and the like by the addition of TS - *dānīm*, Pāṇini designates these suffixes as *vibhakti*. By the application of the rule *na vibhaktau*° the *m* in *dānīm* being a *vibhakti* is not an *iT* and hence will not be dropped. So we can have the form *idānīm* thus:

idam + *dānīm*
iŚ + *dānīm*
i + *dānīm* - *idānīm*

Here the base *idam* is substituted by *iŚ* by the application of the rule *idam iŚ* (*A*.5.3.3) and the *Ś* in *iŚ* is dropped by the rules *halantyam* and *tasya lopaḥ*. From the above it follows that one of the purposes for designating certain *TS*-s as *vibhakti* is to have desired forms like *idānīm*, etc.

2. The second purpose that is served by the designation of the *TS* of this group as *vibhakti* is as follows: the suffix *tasiL* is added to the stem *idam*.

idam + *tas* (IL)
idam + *tas* Ø
iŚ + *tas*
i Ø + *tas* - *itaḥ*

Herein - *tasiL*, *L* is an *iT*, is for the purpose of pronunciation. So the remaining form is - *tas*. The stem *idam* is changed into *i* by the rule *idam iŚ* (*A*.5.3.3) The *Ś* in *iŚ* is dropped (by the rules *halantyam* and *tasya lopaḥ*). Since the suffix *tasiL* is designated as a *vibhakti* the final vowel in - *ta* will have the accent *udātta* by the application of the rule *A*.6.1.171. If - *tasiL* is not designated as a *vibhakti*, then since it is a suffix with *L* as an indicatory letter; the vowel in - *ta* will have the accent *svarita* by the application of the rule - *A*.6.1.193 which is not a desired one.

3. The third purpose in designating the TS of this group as *vibhakti* is as follow: the suffix *tasiL* is added to the pronoun *yad*.

yad + *tas(iL)*
yad + *tas* Ø - *tas*

The *d* in *yad* will be substituted by the letter *a* on the condition that the base *yad* is followed by a *vibhakti*. Since *tasiL* is viewed as a *vibhakti* the letter *d* in *yad* will be changed in to *a*.

ya(d) + *tas*
ya + *tas*
ya + *tas* - *yataḥ*

By the rule *ato guṇe* (A.6.1.97) the *a* in *ya* and *a* will remain as *a*. Thus we arrive at the form *yataḥ*.

Now if the suffix *tas* is not designated as a *vibhakti* then by the rule *tyadādīnāmaḥ* (A.7.2.102) we will not have the substitution *a* for *d* in *yad*. As a result we will not have the form *yataḥ*.

Moreover, the suffixes such as *tasiL*,[15] *traL*[16] and the like respectively convey the senses of the ablative and the locative case-ending. Hence it seems proper to designate them as *vibhakti*.

3.3.3.0 *Suffixes added to Adjectives*

The following are the TS-s which are added to adjectives in order to arrive at adjectival forms conveying the senses of 'more', 'highest degree'.

1. *Superlative*
   1. - *tamaP* - *tama* A.5.3.55
   2. - *iṣṭhaN* - *iṣṭha* A.5.3.55
2. *Comparative*
   1. - *taraP* - *tara* A.5.3.57
   2. - *īyasUN* - *īyas* A.5.3.57

3.3.3.1. *Superlative Suffixes*

These suffixes are generally added to adjectives,[17] to form adjectival stem. In the aphorism *atisāyane tamabiṣṭhanau* (A.5.3.55) it is stated that the suffixes *tamaP* and *iṣṭhaN* are added to the nominal adjectival stems when the senses of highest degree are intended to be conveyed.

For Example:

āḍhya + tamaP
āḍhya + tama - āḍhyatama
and *darśanīyatama*, etc.

Like others suffixes of this group the suffixes - *tamaP* and *iṣṭhaN* too are taken as *svārthika*-suffixes in the sense that they make explicit the meaning that are implied by the bases to which they are added. For example, the expression *āḍhyatamaḥ*. By the base *āḍhya* itself is implied the sense of one who is richest. And this sense is made explicit by the suffix-*tamaP*. Thus the latter is only an indicating factor and not a significant one.[18]

3.3.3.2. *Comparative Suffixes*

In the rule *dvivacana-vibhajyopapade tarabīyasunau* (*A*.5.3.57), it is stated that the suffixes *taraP* - *tara* and *īyasuN* - *īyas* are used to convey the sense of one being superior to the other of the same kind. It is added to an adjectival form or a finite verb. For example, the suffix *taraP* or *īyasUN* is added to the adjectival form *paṭu* to arrive at the adjectival stem *paṭutara* and *paṭīyān* that would convey the sense of one cleverer than the other.

3.3.4. *Verb*

One of the peculiarities of Sanskrit language is the use of comparative and superlative suffixes after finite verb forms. The aphorism - *tiṄaśca* (*A*.5.3.56) states that the superlative and comparative suffixes are added to verbal forms too. For example, *pacatitamām* 'one who cooks exceedingly well'. Here the suffix *tamaP* is added to the base - *pacati* which is a finite verb. Thus verbs also serve as the base for TF. The scope of the application of these suffixes to finite verbs, however, is limited.

3.3.5. *Compound Word*

A TS is mostly applied to a nominal word. But it must be noted that it cannot be applied to any nominal word of one's choice. It should be applied only to those nominal words on the condition that the new forms which would be derived from these words by the addition of the TS are current in usage.

When it is said that the TS-s are added to nominal words, it comes to this that they can be applied to compound words too, as the latter are treated as nominal words. For example, the suffix *cha* - *īya* is added to *dvandva* compound word denoting the day-time associated with the stars *puṣya* and *punarvasu*, as in the case of *tiṣyapunarvasavīyam* (*ahaḥ*).[19]

3.3.6. In some cases we find the indeclinable words such as *yatra, tatra,* etc., and phrases or sentences consisting of *avyaya*-s such as *yathā kathā ca, asti nāsti diṣṭammatiḥ,* etc., serve as bases for TF. Apart from these cases the inflected nominals as well as the nominal stems serve as base for TF.

3.4.. *Summary*

In this chapter an attempt has been made to analyse the *Taddhita*-suffixes in relation to their morphological characteristics; and, the entire TS-s have been classified into six groups. Each group consists of a general suffix, along with some exceptions and also conditioned by specific lexemes. However, the sixth group of suffixes belongs to the miscellaneous ones, which unlike the earlier group of suffixes does not have exceptions invariably. Further it has been set forth that the bases for the TS-s are nominal words and stems; while the bases for case-endings are stems only.[20] Such a specific base for the TS-s is obtained from the rule *A* 4.1.82. Thus for the TS-s we have two types of bases, namely, a nominal word and a stem. As far as the *asvārthika*-type of suffixes are concerned a nominal word serves as a base, and for the *svārthika*-type, the nominal stems too serve as bases. Moreover, pronouns, verbs and adjectives too serve as bases in limited cases.

In the following chapter we shall deal with the syntactic features that are involved in *TF*.

REFERENCES

1. See Sec. 1-7-1 of the present work.
2. See *SK.* on *A*.4.2.92 and also *Kāśika. ibid.*
3. This is suggested by Chaturvedi, S.P. in *Sārasvatasandarśana.*
4. The following four meanings are listed in *A*.4.2.67-70.
   (i) The resultant form signifies a country bearing the name of its *prakṛti* by the addition of the suffix - *aṆ*. It is so because the country consists of the sense of the *prakṛti* in abundance.

(ii) accomplished by him (*A*.4.2.68)
(iii) a residence (*A*.4.2.69)
(iv) situated not far from a particular place (*A*.4.2.70).

5. See *SK.* on *A*.4.1.92.
6. Here the suffix - *aṆ* is added to the word *paraśavya* after the deletion of the suffix-*yaT* which is a part of the base. The word is formed thus:
   paraśu + *cha* + *aṆ*
   paraśu + Ø + *a*
   parasav + *a* - *paraśavaḥ*
7. Here the suffix *yaÑ* is added to the word *kaṁsīya* after the deletion of the suffix-*cha* which is a part of the base. The word is formed thus:
   kaṁsa + *cha* + *yaÑ*
   kaṁsa + Ø + *ya*
   kaṁśyaḥ
8. Here the suffix - *aṆ* is enjoined along with the deletion of the suffix which is a part of the base.
9. This is also a phonologically conditioned suffix.
10. There are only six feminine suffixes, namely, *ṄiP, ṄīṢ, ṄīN, TāP, DāP* and *CāP*, which come under this group.
11. *kṛttaddhitasamāsāśca* (*A*.1.2.47)
12. Pāṇini's *Taddhita-affixation Rules*, p. 2.
13. *atyantasvārthikānām subutpatteḥ pūrvameva pravṛttiḥ-Udyota* on *MBh. A*.4.1.48.
14. S.C. Vasu, *Aṣṭādhyāyī* on *A*.5.3.1.
15. *A*.5.3.7.
16. *A*.5.3.10.
17. These are added to verbs too. See *A*.5.3.56.
18. *atiśayitari vidyamānāt prātipadikāt svārtha tamaP iṣṭhaN ca syādityarthaḥ*, Bālamanoramā, on *A*.5.3.55.
19. *dvandvācchaḥ* (*A*.4.2.6)
20. See *A*.4.1.1.

CHAPTER - IV

SYNTACTIC FEATURES INVOLVED IN TADDHITA-FORMATION

4.0. *Introduction*

The derivational system of Sanskrit language is syntax-based. According to tradition, complex words in Sanskrit are derived from their Underlying Sentence (*US*). That is to say, each derived word in Sanskrit has in general an US at its base.[1] The derived word and the US are mostly synonymous. Thus the compound words and the words derived by the addition of derivational suffixes are based on the US excepting in a few cases. In the present chapter we will discuss the *Taddhita* (Formation) suffixation and the Syntactic Features involved in the latter.

To begin with, we shall discuss the classification of the derivational type of suffixation and compounding from the stand-point of syntax.

4.0.1. *The Syntactic and Lexical Derivation*

The derivational type of suffixation and compounding when viewed from the stand-point of Syntax may be classified into two:

1. Certain words can be used as such as also in the form of their US. For example, *rājapuruṣaḥ*, 'the King's servant'. It can be used as such and also in the form *rājñaḥ puruṣaḥ*. That is, the word *rājapuruṣaḥ* and the expression *rājñaḥ puruṣaḥ* can be used interchangeably. This type allows room for the alternative use of a compound word. Pāṇini's rule *vibhāṣā* (*A*.2.1.11) takes care of this type of compounding. The compounding which is derived from its US is traditionally known as *anitya samāsa* 'alternative compounding'. Thus in Sanskrit we may employ

either the derived word or its US. This type of derivation may be characterised as *Syntactic Derivation;* and

2. Certain words can be used only in their derived forms and not in the form of their US. This type of derivation is known as obligatory derivation. There are two types of obligatory derivations, namely, (a) *asvapadavigraha,* and (b) *avigraha* which may be explained as follows:

(a) *asvapadavigraha*

i. There are certain compound words which are derived from their US and which do not convey the meaning of the latter; and

ii. There are some other words which while conveying their senses identical with those of their US are structurally different from one another. In this case, the US cannot be used optionally in the place of the derived word.

These two types of words are known as *asvapada vigraha,* and they may be illustrated as follows:

i. *Khaṭvāruḍhaḥ*[2] one who is recklessly audacious. Here the US is *khatvām ārūḍhaḥ* - 'one who moves up and occupies a bed'. Semantically the above US is not an equivalent of the output. So neither can be used in the place of another. Linguistically such a type of derivation, that is, compounding is called lexicalised form. The lexicalisation may occur due to the semantic, morphological idiosyncratic nature of the output.[3] The present case is an example of semantically lexicalised form in view of the absence of similarity between the semantic reading and its US.

ii. *Upakṛṣṇam* 'near Krishna'. Here the US is *kṛṣṇasya samīpam.* In this case the derived word does not possess all the words which are found in the US. Though semantically the derived word and the US are similar, yet these two cannot be used interchangeably. This type of *asvapadavigraha* derivation is also treated as an obligatory one.[4] Linguistically such types of forms come under the purview of morphologically lexicalised form.

(b) *avigraha:* This type of derivation cannot be used as an alternative to its US. For example, *kumbhakāraḥ.* Here there is an Analytical Sentence (AS) *kumbham karoti* or grammatical structure which appears as a US but is not used in the place of the output. This AS is useful only for grammatical analysis and is traditionally known as *alaukika vigrahavākya*. It is almost morphologically and semantically similar to the output; and it is not being used as an alternate form to the output on the ground that it is not found in current usage [*anabhidhānāt*].

While discussing the restrictions on productivity, Bauer, L. lays down certain pragmatic restriction on WFRs. Here the first and the foremost factor is the 'Requirement of existence' which deals with the existence of the derived word in actual usage. Though by the application of the grammatical rules we can derive any number of words, yet since actual occurrence is a pre-requisite for the usage of the derived word in a lanugage, any derived word cannot be used.[5] Exactly similar consideration applies to the *avigrahava* type of derivation too which we have explained earlier.

Thus the two types of obligatory derivation may be referred to as either Lexical derivation or non-syntactic derivation.

We shall now discuss these classifications in regard to TF.

4.1. *The Syntactic and Lexical Derivation in TF*

In TF, the US of the derived word is used optionally. Mostly the *asvārthika*[6] type of *Taddhita*-suffixation has its own US which is used in the place of the derived word. Here the semantic reading of the derived word is the source for the latter. This type of formation may be characterised as Syntactic Derivation. It further proves that a word that is derived from its US is syntax-based. For example, *aupagavaḥ*. Here the US is *upagorapatyam* 'descendant of upagu'. By the rule *tasyāpatyam* (*A*.4.1.92) the suffix - *aṆ* is added to the nominal word, namely, *upagoḥ*. By the rule *samarthānāmprathamād vā* (*A*.4.1.82) the - *aṆ* suffix is added optionally to the first word of its syntactic string (US), that is, the word which is syntactically and semantically connected with other words. This rule provides room for a speaker to use either the derived word or its US. In the above instance, the derived word *aupagavaḥ* can be used as such or in the form of its US, namely, *upagorapatyam* rather interchangeably. In a similar manner all the *asvārthika* types of TF may be deduced from their own US-s which can also be used.

There are some other *Taddhita*-Formations called *svārthika-s* which do not have any US. They, however, have *AS*-s which resemble the *US*-s or *vigrahavākya*-s. But those *AS*-s are not employed in current usage. These types of words are traditionally known as *nitya-taddhita*-s or 'obligatory *Taddhita*-Formation'. That is, unlike the *asvārthika* type of formations, here the *AS* is not used as its alternative. Such kind of formations may be characterized as the lexical derivation, as the formation takes place within the lexicon. For example, the *svārthika* suffixes, namely - *tamaP* and - *iṣṭhaN* are added to the nominal bases namely *āḍhya* and *paṭu* respectively enabling one to arrive at the formations *āḍhyatamaḥ* 'richest' and *patisthaḥ* 'most skilled'. Here the above suffixes merely indicate that the bases *āḍhya* and *paṭu* contain within themselves the senses of 'most affluent' and 'most efficious' respectively. [*atiśayena āḍhyaḥ / atiśayena paṭuḥ*]. Similarly in *aśvakaḥ* and *gardabhakaḥ* the *svārthika* suffix *ka* merely indicates that the bases *aśva* 'horse' and *gardabha* 'ass' the used in the sense of *kutsita* 'wickedness' (*kutsitaḥ asvaḥ, kutsitaḥ gardabhaḥ*). In the above cases we find that the AS-s of the derived words are similar to US-s or *vigrahavākya*. But these AS-s are not used in the place of the derived words. As observed[7] by Joshi "Although we have here strings expressing the same meaning they are strictly in grammar, given for the purpose of explaining the corresponding affixed forms; they are not so used in actual language". Moreover unlike the *asvārthika*-type of formation here the AS is not a source for derivation. In the case of the *asvārthika*-types of formations the US acts as a source of derivation. By the rule *A*.4.1.82 the *Taddhita*-suffixes are to be added to the first nominal word of the US optionally. On the contrary the *svārthika* types of suffixes are added to the nominal bases directly. The bases will be specified in the *Taddhita*-Formation Rules themselves. Here the US is not used to derive the new word. Since the formation takes place within the lexicon without having its US, it may be characterised as Lexical Derivation or non-syntactic derivation. Thus the *Taddhita*-Formation also may be broadly classified syntactically into two major categories, namely, (1) Syntactic derivation [which is based on the US]; and (2) Lexical non-syntactic derivation which is not based on the US.

4.2. *Syntactic Derivation*

4.2.0. The words that are derived by the addition of *asvārthika* type of *Taddhita* suffixes have a special feature in this that they convey the *Kāraka*-relation through their underlying structure excepting in the cases of words involving the genitive case-ending. For example, words such as *vaiyākaraṇaḥ* 'a grammarian' and the like which are of *asvārthika* types convey the relation of *karma* through the underlying structure, namely *vyākaranamadhīte.* As explained above the *asvārthika* types of *Taddhita*-formations have their own underlying structures from which the words are derived. Here Pāṇini records several types of underlying structures to derive new words. These underlying structures not only act as the sources for the derivation but also provide us with an appropriate semantic reading of the latter. Moreover in these US-s the *Kāraka*-relations are explicitly stated.[8]

4.2.1. *The Scope of the Present Analysis*

The purpose of the present section is to analyse the various *Kāraka* (syntactic) relations which are involved in the underlying sentences of the derived words. And such an analysis is necessary to get the appropriate meaning of the output. It is because sometimes in the *Taddhita*-Formation, one and the same suffix conveys a variety of meanings and the same output stands for manifold senses. Based upon the *Kāraka* role of the base with the suffix the exact meaning of the output is determined. For example, the word *sraughnaḥ* has the following underlying structures, namely,

srughnasya apatyam = sraughnaḥ
srughnād āgataḥ = sraughnaḥ
srughne bhavaḥ = sraughnaḥ

Here to derive the word *sraughnaḥ* we may use any one of the above underlying structures with the appropriate case-ending. These underlying case-ending alongwith *kṛt*- endings give the exact semantic reading of the output. For instance in the case of *srugnād āgataḥ* 'one who comes from srugna village' the underlying ablative case-ending expresses the *apādāna kāraka* relation (that is, the source from which the object is moving). In the surface level the word *sraughnaḥ* is capable of conveying manifold senses. Its specific meaning can be identified on the basis of the analysis of the different US-s from which it is derived. In short in the absence of such an analysis the semantic reading of the output is difficult to attain.

4.2.1.2. We have earlier said there is an US for representing the *Kāraka*-relation in the case of *asvārthika*-type of word. The TS-s are generally added to nominal words (*subanta*-s) which do not directly represent the *Kāraka*-relation; for, the signification of a *Kāraka*-relation is based upon the relation of a noun to a verb. This is precisely the reason for defining *Kāraka* as *Kriyānvayī* that is, 'that which is related to a verb / action'. In TF, the suffixes are added to nominal words, and hence they do not possess any *Kāraka*-relation at the surface level.

Generally the *Kāraka* theory rules explain syntactic relations though the assignment of appropriate inflectional case-endings. For example, *vyākaraṇam paṭhati*, 'one who studies grammar'. Here the inflectional suffix - *am* is attached to the nominal stem, namely, *vyākaraṇa* to represent the *karma-kāraka*-relation according to the rule of *anabhihite* (A.2.3.1) and *karmani dvitiyā* (A.2.3.2)` Here there are two processes which take place simultaneously to represent the *karma-kāraka*-relation, and they are: the process through which the rule *karturīpsitatamam karma* (A.1.4.49) assigns the designation *karma* to the nominal stem; and, then the process through which the second case suffix is assigned to the nominal stem which possesses the designation *karma*.

By these processes the inflectional case-endings represent the *Kāraka*-relations on the basis of the designation that the nominal stem possesses. It should be noted here that the designations are assigned to the nominal stems on the basis of the relation of nominal stem to the verb. In the above instances, the nominal stem *vyākaraṇa* serves as an object of the corresponding action namely 'reading'. Thus by the rule *A.*1.4.43 the designation *karma* is assigned to the stem *vyākaraṇa* which, in turn, receives the second case-ending assigned to the stem which possesses the *karma* designation by the rule *A.*2.3.2.

As far as the *Taddhita*-formation is concerned Pāṇini directly assigns the appropriate case-endings which determine the appropriate *kāraka*-relations without assigning any designations to the nominal stems. Here we can only assume the appropriate *Kāraka*-relations on the basis of the underlying case-endings. It should be borne in mind here that the underlying case-endings represent some *Kāraka*-relations, only when they are associated with a verb/action. It is because the inflectional case-endings are assigned even in the absence of verbs also as in the case of *upapadavibhaktis.* Here we do not have any *Kāraka*-relation apart from the mere addition of case-affixes. For example, *gurave namaḥ.* Here the dative case-ending is assigned to the nominal stem *guru* owing to the usage of word *namaḥ* in juxtaposition to it. Thus the assumption of the appropriate *Kāraka*-relation is based upon the underlying case-endings which are conditioned/ governed by a verb/ action. For example, the second case-ending is generally used to express the *karma-kāraka* relation, by the rules *anabhihite* (*A.*2.3.1) and *karmaṇi dvitīyā* (*A.*2.3.2). By this process the inflectional case-endings excepting nominative and genitive case-endings (which come under the domain of *anabhihita* 'that which is unexpressed by the other factors)[9] represent the six *Kāraka*-relations.[10] Thus in *Taddhita*-formations we can assume that the second case ending when associated with a verb/action in an underlying structure would normally represent the *karma-kāraka* rclation on the basis of the general *kāraka* rule *karmaṇi dvitīyā* (*A*.2.3.2). Similarly we can assume all the *Kāraka*-relations on the basis of their respective case-endings that are assigned in the *Kāraka* rules. Apart from this the nominal case-ending is used when the appropriate *Kāraka*-relations are expressed through the other factors. The base to which the suffixes are added will be specified by an appropriate case-ending. The base along with the case-endings are specified in the *Taddhita*-formation rules themselves.

We shall now discuss the different types of US-s from which the *Kāraka* relations are noticed. To begin with, the second case-ending associated with a verb expresses the *karma-kāraka* relation. It may be added here that in TF we notice two types of bases (words) used to represent the syntactic connection with the other word in the given US.

1. The pronoun *tat* with various case-endings is often used to refer to the base in general. For example *tasyāpatyam* (*A*.4.1.92) *tena raktam rāgāt* (*A*.4.2.1) *tadadhite tadveda* (*A*.4.2.59) etc. Herein the genitive, instrumental and accusative pronominal words stand for any base with the given case-ending in general, and they convey the syntactic connection of the base with the other words of the US, namely, *apatyam*, *raktam* and *adhīte*.

2. In some other cases the bases with different case-endings are restricted to specific lexemes and this shows their syntactic connection with the other words in a US. For example, *nakṣatreṇa yuktaḥ kālaḥ* 'the day when the moon is in conjunction with a star' (*A*.4.2.3), *somamarhati yaḥ* 'deserving soma' (*A*.4.4.137), etc. Herein the words *nakṣatra* and *soma* ending with instrumental and accusative case-suffixes respectively stand only for the specific lexemes referred in the rules mentioned above. Thus in TF we find two types of bases with different case-endings which bring in their syntactic connection with the other word in the US-s.

In the following cases the assusative case-ending word which is the first member of US serves as a base for TS.

Rule	*Example*	*Meaning*
1. tadadhīte tadveda *A*.4.2.59-66	vyākaranamadhīte, veda vā-vaiyākaraṇaḥ	'a grammarian'
2. tadgacchati pathi dūtayoḥ *A*.4.3.85-89	mathurām gacchati - māthuraḥ	'a road/messenger going to Mathura'
3. tatpratianupū-rva° *A*.4.4.28-46	pratīpam vartate-prātīpikaḥ	'moving against the current'
4. tadvahati rathayuga° *A*.4.4.76-86	ratham vahati-rathyaḥ	'which draws the chariot'
5. somamarhati yaḥ *A*.4.4.137-38	somamarhati soṃyaḥ	'deserving soma' [fit for participating in a sacrifice]
6. taddharati, vahati° *A*.5.1.50-55	vaṁśabhāram harati vahati āvahati-vāmśa-bhārikaḥ	'who carries/ conveys/brings a load of bamboos'
7. tadarhati *A*.5.1.63-76	śatamarhati - śatikaḥ, śatyaḥ	'deserving hundred pieces'
8. tamadhiṣṭo bhṛto° *A*.5.1.80-92	māsam adhiṣṭaḥ bhṛtaḥ bhūtaḥ bhāvī-māsikaḥ	'a. invited to teach for a month b. hired, c. lasted d. will last for a month'
9. tadasya brahmacar-yam[11] *A*.5.1.94	māsam brahmacar-yam asya - māsikam	'who practices continence for a period of one month'
10. tadarham *A*.5.1.117	rājānamarhati-rājavat	'deserving the king'
11. tat sarvādeḥ *A*.5.2.7	sarvapatham vyāp-noti-sarvapathīnaḥ	'covering the entire route'

12.aṁśaṁ hārī A.5.2.69	aṁśaṁ hārī-aṁśakaḥ	'legal heir'
13.śitoṣṇābhyām kāriṇī A.5.2.72	śītam karotiśītakaḥ	'a lazy man'
14.śrotriyam chando'dhite. A.5.2.84	chandaḥ adhīte-śrotriyaḥ	'one who studies the Veda'

In the following cases the Instrumental case-ending word which is the first member of the given US serves as a base for TS.

Rule	*Example*	*Meaning*
1. tena raktam rāgāt A.4.2.1-13	kaṣāyeṇa raktam vastram-kāṣāyam	'a cloth dyed with red colour'
2. nakṣatreṇa yuktaḥ kālaḥ A.4.2.3	puṣyeṇa yuktaḥ kālaḥ-pauṣyaḥ	'the day when the moon is in conjunction with the star Puṣya'
3. (tena)[12] dṛṣṭam sāma	vasiṣṭena dṛṣṭam sāma-vāsiṣṭam	'sāma intuitively felt by vasiṣṭa'
4. tena nirvṛttam (kartā) A.4.3.68	kuśāmbena nirvṛttā nagārī-kauśambī kuśāmba'.	'a city built or completed by Kuśamba'
5. tenaproktam (kartā) A.4.3.101-111	māthureṇa proktam-māthurī vṛttiḥ	'expounded by Māthura'
6. tenaikadik A.4.3.112-119	sudāmnā eka dik-saudāminī (vidyut)	'lightning that moves in the direction of the mount Sudāmam
7. tena dīvyati khanati A.4.4.2-27	akṣaiḥ dīvyati khanati-ākṣikaḥ	'one who gambles' 'one who digs with a spade, etc'.
8. gṛhapatinā samyukte Ñyaḥ A.4.4.90-91	gṛhapatinā samyuktaḥ(agniḥ)-gārhapatyaḥ	'the domestic (fire) maintained by the sacrificer'

9. pūrvaiḥ kṛtam (kartā) *A*.4.4.133-35	pūrvaiḥ kṛtam-pūrvyaḥ pūrvīnaḥ	'practised by ancestors'
10.tena krītam	śatenakrītaḥ-śatyaḥ	'purchased by paying hundred (rupees)'
11.uttarapathe nāhṛtaṁ ca *A*.5.1.77	uttarapathenā-hṛtam-auttarapa-thikam	'brought through the northern route'
12.tena nirvṛttam. *A*.5.1.79	ahnānirvṛttam-ahnikam	'completed or accomplished within a day'
13.tena parijayya labhya° *A*.5.1.93	māsena parijayyaḥ labhyaḥ-māsikam	'conquered or gained, within a month'
14.tena yathā kạthā° *A*.5.1.98-99	hastena diyate-hastyam	'it is given or done by hand'
15.tena tulyam kriyāced°[13] *A*.5.1.115-118	brāhmanena tulyam vartate-brahmanavat	'resembles a brahmin'
16.vrātena jīvati *A*.5.2.21-22	vrātena jīvati-vrātīnaḥ	'he who lives by strenuous physical labour'
17.tena vittaḥ *A*.5.2.26	vidyayā vittaḥ vidyā-cuñcuḥ	'well-known or renowned by knowledge'
18.sasyena-parijātaḥ *A*.5.2.68	sasyena parijātaḥ -sasyakaḥ	'possessed of ethical excellences'
19.pārśvenānvi-cchāti *A*.5.2.75-79	pārśvenānvicchati-pārśvikaḥ	'one who seeks to gain something by fraudulent means'

In the following two cases we notice the Dative case ending word as the first member of the US.

1. tasmai hitam[14] *A*.5.1.5	vatsebhyaḥ hitaḥ-vatsīyaḥ	'one who brings good to the calves'

2. tasmaiprabha-vati *A*.5.1.101	santapaya prabhavati sāntāpikaḥ	'he who inflicts suffering'

In the following cases we notice Ablative case-ending word as the first members of the US.

1. tata agataḥ *A*.4.3.74-84	srughnādāgataḥ sraughnaḥ	'arrived from srughna'
2. dharmapa-thyartha *A*.4.4.92	dharmādanapetam-dharmyam	'not swerving from righteousness'
3. tantrādacirā-dapahṛte *A*.5.2.70	tantrādacirādapa-hṛtaḥ tantrakaḥ	'cloth brought fresh from the loom'

In the following cases, we notice Locative case-ending word as a first member of an US.

1. tatroddhṛtam *A*.4.2.14-20	śarāve uddhṛtaḥ śārāvaḥ	'rice taken from and placed in dishes'
2. tatra jātaḥ *A*.4.3.25-51	srughne jātaḥ sraughnaḥ	'he who is born in *Srughna*'
3. tatra bhavaḥ *A*.4.3.53-73	srughnebhavaḥ sraughnaḥ	'that which exists in *Srughna*'
4. tatra niyuktaḥ *A*.4.4.69-74	śulkaśālāyām niyuktaḥ-śaulka-śālikaḥ	'he who is employ-ed to guard the custom house'
5. nikaṭe vasati *A*.4.4.73	nikaṭe vasati-naikaṭikaḥ	'one who lives near (a village)'
6. tatra sādhuḥ *A*.4.4.98-119	karmaṇi sādhuḥ karmaṇyaḥ	'dexterous in action'
7. tatra vidita iti *A*.5.1.96-97	sarvabhūmau viditaḥ sarvabhaumaḥ	'world-renowned'
8. tatra ca dīyate *A*.5.1.96-97	māse dīyate-māsikam	'that which is given or to be done in a month'
9. tatra tasyeva *A*.5.1.116	mathurāyāmiva-mathuravat	'that which is similar the one in Mathurā'

10.karmaṇi ghaṭo' ṭhaC *A*.5.2.35	karmaṇi ghaṭati karmathaḥ	'zealously engaged inthe performance of activities'
11.tatra kuśalaḥ[15] pathaḥ	pathikusalaḥ pathakaḥ	'he who knows the features of a place'

Earlier we have said that the *asvārthika*-type of TF besides having US expresses the *Kāraka*-relations too excepting the genitive case-ending. We shall now discuss the genitive case-ending word and its role in TF.

Words like *dāśarathiḥ* which are of *asvārthika*-type do not convey any *Kāraka* relation but only a relation in a general manner, namely, the relation of the one who possesses to the one possessed. This sense of relation is different from the *Kāraka*-relation. In these cases, the genitive case-ending word is the base for the derivation of a new word. In other words, the first word of the US is a genitive case-ending one. Here we do not find any particular *kāraka*-relation such as *karma*, *karaṇa*, etc.

Pāṇini prescribes the usage of the genitive case-ending to signify the relation of one factor to another which is not a verb. It must be noted here that there will definitely be a relation in one manner or another between a word in the genitive case-ending and the verb in a sentence. But that relation will be an indirect one. So Pāṇini prescribes the usage of the genitive case-ending to signify the relation between two nouns in a sentence. In this sense, the genitive case-ending serves the purpose of signifying all relations excepting those that involve the relation between a noun and a verb [that is, the *kriyā-kāraka* relation]. For example, *rājñaḥ puruṣaḥ*, 'a king's servant'. Here the genitive case-ending conveys the relation between the king and the servant; it does not signify any *kāraka* relation.

The first and the foremost meaning of the genitive case-ending is 'possession' in a wide sense, which includes any of the following intimate relations,[16] namely,

> One's son, house, servant, books or works, wife, father, uncle, master, pictures (which he has bought or painted), enemies, life, opinions and portrait.

Apart from these Pāṇini sometimes employs the subjective genitive (*kartari ṣaṣṭhī*) and objective-gentive (*karmaṇi saṣṭhī*) as in the case of *bhavataḥ śāyikā* 'your turn to lie down', *apām sraṣṭā* 'creator of waters', etc. In these cases the genitive case-ending denote the subject-object relation by the rule *kartṛ karmaṇoḥ kṛti* (A.2.3.65). We find similar constructions in English also. As explained[17] by Jesperson "the use of subjective and 'objective' can be shown by such series as:

> (possessive-subjective) a girl's (or her) heart, mind, will, illness, feeling, admiration.
> (possessive-objective) a man's (or his) sons, friends, heirs, pupils, successors, followers, admirers."

Thus the genitive case-ending plays a vital role to explain the relations other than the *Kāraka-s.*

In TF we find both the types construction, namely, possessive and its extended relations and also the relation between a noun and verb/action in specific senses.

In the following cases the genitive case-ending word serves as a base for TS-s.

Rule	*Example*	*Meaning*
1.tasyāpatyam A.4.1.92-176	daśarathasya apatyam-dāśarathiḥ	'descendent of Daśaratha'
2.tasya samūhaḥ A.4.2.37-54	kākānām samūhaḥ-kākam	'flight of crows'
3.tasya nivāsaḥ A.4.2.69-70	śibīnāṁ nivāsaḥ deśaḥ-śaibaḥ	'a residence of Śibi-s'
4.tasya vyākhyāna° A.4.3.66-73	supām vyākhyānaḥ-saupaḥ	'a commentary on declensional suffixes'
5.tasyedam	srughnasyedam	'belonging to srughna'
6.tasya vikāraḥ A.4.3.134-168	ikṣūṇām vikāraḥ, avayavaḥ-aikṣavaḥ	'a modification or a limb of sugarcane'
7.tasya dharmyam A.4.4.47-50	śulkaśalāyāḥ dharmyam-śaulkaśālikaḥ	'the duty that one should do at a custom-house'

8. hṛdayasya priyaḥ *A*.4.4.95.96	hṛdayasyapriyaḥ-hṛdyaḥ	'dear to one's heart'
9. dūtasyabhaga° *A*.4.4.120	dūtāsyabhāgaḥ karma vā - dūtyaḥ dūtyam	'role to function of an ambassador'
10. rakṣoyātū-nām° *A*.4.4.121-122	raksasām hananī-rakṣasya	'he who kills the demon'
11. asurasyasvam° *A*.4.4.123-124	asurasyasvam-asuryam	'property of an asura'
12. śiva-samariṣṭasya° *A*.4.4.143-144	śivasyakareḥ sivatātiḥ	'making auspicious favourable'
13. tasya nimittam° *A*.5.1.38-41	śatasyanimittam dhanapatina sam-yogaḥ śatyaḥ śatikaḥ	'an understanding with a rich man for the loan of a hundred pieces'
14. tasyeśvaraḥ *A*.5.1.42	pṛthivyā iśvaraḥ-pārthivaḥ	'a king/emperor'
15. tasya vāpaḥ *A*.5.1.45	prasthasya vāpaḥ-prāsthikam	'(a field) sown with a quantity of seed measuring a prastha'
16. tasya ca dakṣiṇā° *A*.5.9.95	agniṣṭomasya dakṣiṇā āgniṣṭomikī	'sacrificial fee for the Agniṣṭoma sacrifice'
17. tatra tasyeva *A*.5.1.116	rāmasyaivarāmavat	'resembling rama'
18. tasya bhāva-stvastvatalau *A*.5.1.119-136	aśvasyabhāvaḥ-aśvatvam, aśvatā	'the state/nature or condition of being a horse or horseness'
19. dhānyanāṁ bhavane° *A*.5.2.1	mudgānām bhava-nam kṣetram -maudgīnam	'a field in which Mung beans are grown'
20. yathamukha° *A*.5.2.6	yathamukhasya darśanaḥ yāthā-mukhīnaḥ	'one who looks straight at mirror'

21. tasyapāka-mule° *A*.5.2.24	pilūnam pākaḥ-pīlukunaḥ	'season for the ripening of the pīlu fruits'
22. tasyapūraṇe-ḍat *A*.5.2.48	ekādaśanām pūraṇaḥ ekādaśa	'eleventh'

Nominative

According to Pāṇini the nominative case-ending signifies the meaning, the gender and the number of the stem to which it is added. It also signifies the sense of measure which is the significance of the nominal stem. These may be illustrated as follows:

a. *Uccaih* 'high'. Here the suffix - *suP* is added to the indeclinable stem *Uccais* to denote the meaning of the stem. That is the suffix conveys nothing more than the meaning of the stem.

b. Three kinds of suffixes are added to a nominal stem to signify the masculine, the feminine and the neuter gender. These are noticed respectively in the cases of words such as *Vṛkṣaḥ* 'a tree', *Kumārī* 'a girl' and *vanam* 'a forest'. In these cases, the suffix -*suP* is added to the stems to denote mainly the genders of the respective stems.

c. *Droṇaḥ* - 'a specific kind of measure'. Here the - *suP* is added to the stem *droṇa* to denote the sense of measure - the sense that is conveyed by the stem itself.

d. The words *ekaḥ* 'one', *dvau*, 'two', *bahavaḥ* 'many' respectively contain the suffixes *sU*, *au* and *Jas*. These convey the senses of singular, dual and plural numbers, the senses that are conveyed by their stems themselves.

2. Whenever the Kāraka-relations are expressed through other factors such as (a) *tiṄ*, (b) *Kṛt*, (c) *taddhita* and also through compound words, then the Nominative case-ending will be used.[18] This is applicable to all *Kāraka*-s. That is, when the *Kāraka*-relations are not expressed through other factors, then only in those cases the appropriate case-ending will be used to represent the respective *Kāraka*-relations. This may be

made clear by making a reference to the *Kāraka*-relation of *karman* which denotes the direct object. A simple sentence which may be arrived at from the base is: *kumbha + aṁ kṛñ + ti* - *kumbham karoti* 'he makes a pot'. Here the *Kāraka*-relation, namely, the *kartā* alone is conveyed by the verbal suffix *ti* in *karoti* and not the direct object *kumbha*. By the rules *anabhihite* (*A*.2.3.1) and *karmaṇi dvitīyā* (*A*.2.3.2) the accusative case-ending is added to the stem *kumbha* since the object, namely, *kumbha* is not expressed through the verbal suffix, namely *ti* in *karoti*. If the object is signified by the verbal suffix as in the case of *kriyate*, etc., then the nominative case-ending would be added to the object. For example, *kumbhaḥ kriyate*.

We shall now furnish examples to prove this in regard to the remaining *kāraka*-s also, when they are expressed by other factors. In the case of *snānīyam cūrnam* 'powder fit to be used for bathing' since the sense of instrument pertaining to *cūrṇa* has been already expressed by the *kṛt* suffix-*anīya* (*A*.3.3.113), the instrumental case-ending is not added to the stem *cūrṇa*. But in the expression *cūrṇena snāti* 'he takes bath by using powder', the instrumental case-ending is added to *cūrṇa*, as the sense of instrument is not conveyed by the *kṛt*-suffix.

In *dānīyo vipraḥ* 'a brahmin to whom something is offered', since the *sampradāna* has already been expressed by the *kṛt* suffix - *anīya* (*A*.3.3.113), the dative case-ending is not added to the stem *vipra* 'a brahmin'. But in *viprāya (gāṁ) dadāti*, the verbal suffix *ti* in *dadāti* does not signify *sampradāna*. Therefore, the dative case-ending is added to *vipra*.

In *prapatanaḥ parvataḥ* 'a mountain from which one falls', since the sense of *apādāna* has already been expressed by the *kṛt* suffix-*ana* (*A*.3.3.113) the ablative case-ending is not added to the stem *parvata*. But in the expression *parvatāt patati* 'he falls from a mountain', the ablative case-ending is added to the stem *parvata* as the sense of *apādāna* is not conveyed by the verbal suffix. This is an example of nominative *apādāna*.

Similarly, *vīrapuruṣako grāmaḥ* 'a village containing heroic persons' is an example of nominative location. Here the *bahuvrīhi*-compound denotes the sense of *adhikaraṇa* and hence we do not have the locative case-ending to the stem *grāmaḥ*. But in the expression *grāme vīrāḥ puruṣāḥ*, the locative case-ending is added to the stem *grāma* as the sense of *adhikaraṇa* is not conveyed by any other source.

In the TF, we find the use of the nominative case-ending word as the first member in an US. For example, *indro devatā asya - aindram (haviḥ)*. Here in the US the word *indraḥ* is a nominative case-ending one. In the derived word *aindra* the suffix - *aṆ* is added to the word *indraḥ* to denote the sense that Indra is the deity to whom the sacrificial substance is offered. Thus the output *aindram* denotes the sense of the sacrificial substance which is not the sense of any of the words of the US. It should be noted here that wherever the nominative ending word is used as a base in TF, the output refers generally to an object that is not the sense of any of the words of the US. Here, however, the meaning of the output is denoted by the genitive case-ending. In the present case the meaning of the output, namely, *aindram* is *asya devatā* 'the deity for which a sacrificial offering or a hymn is intended'. This type of formation resembles an exocentric construction as in the case of *bahuvrīhi*-compound. Thus, where the nominative case-ending word acts as the base, we invariably find the occurrence of the other case-ending word to denote the meaning of the output. In the following cases the Nominative case-ending word which is a first member of the US acts as a base for *Taddhita*-suffixes.

Rules	***Example***	***Meaning***
1.sā'sminpaurṇa° A.4.2.21-23	pauṣī paurṇamasīasmin- pauṣaḥ	'the month in which the full-moon day is associated with *puṣya* star'
2.sāsya devatā A.4.2.24-25	indro devatā asya - aindram	'a sacrificial offering of which Indra is the deity'
3.so'syādiriti° A.4.2.55	paṅkti radirasya pragāthasya- paṅktaḥ	'a *ṛk* which begins with a *paṅkti* metre'

4. saṁgrāme° A.4.2.56	subhadrā prayojanam asya saṁgrāmasya-saubhadraḥ	'the war waged for attaining Subhadrā'
5. tadasyam°	daṇḍaḥ praharaṇam A.4.2.57 (krīḍāyām)-dāṇḍā	'a game in which asyām stumps are used as instrument'
6. tadasmin° A.4.2.67	udumbarāḥ asmin deśe santi-audambaraḥ	'name of the place abounding in *udumbara* trees'
7. tadasya soḍham A.4.3.52	niśā soḍham asya adhyayanasya-naiśaḥ	'a pupil who is accustomed to study at night'
8. so'syanivāsaḥ A.4.3.89-100.	mathurā nirvāsaḥ asya- māthuraḥ	'resident of Mathurā'
9. tadasya paṇyam A.4.4.51-65	apūpaḥ paṇyam asya-āpūpikaḥ	'a dealer in cakes'
10. tadasmai° A.4.4.66-68	agrabhojanam asmai niyuktam dīyate-āgrabhojanikaḥ	'entitled to be served with food first'
11. padamasmin° A.4.4.87	padamasmin (kardame) dṛśyam-padyaḥ	'swampy ground which is not completely deprived of moisture and wherein footprints are clearly seen'
12. mūlamasyābarhi	mūlam eṣām (māṣāṇām ābarhi) A.4.4.88	'the plants that are to be plucked along with - mūlyaḥ their roots'
13. tadvānāsām° A.4.4.125-26	varcasvān upadhāno mantraḥ āsām iṣṭa-kānām-varcsyaḥ	'the orderly arrangement of the hymn containing the word varcas'
14. tadasya° A.5.1.16	prākāraḥ āsām iṣṭakānam syāt-prākārīyaḥ	'the bricks with which a wall can be built'

15. tadasmin° *A*.5.1.47-49	pañca asmin vṛddhiḥ diyate-pañcakaḥ	'one to whom the amount which is five times more than what is received as debt is given'
16. so'syāṁś° *A*.5.1.56	pañca aṁśaḥ asya - pañcakaḥ	'that which consists of five parts'
17. tadasya° *A*.5.1.57-62	prasthaḥ parimāṇam asya-prāsthikaḥ (rāśiḥ)	'a heap measuring one prastha'
18. samayastad° *A*.5.1.104-114	samayaḥ prāptaḥ asya-sāmayikam	'(an action) for taking which the opportune moment has come'
19. tadasya° *A*.5.2.36-38	tārakāḥ sañjātaḥ asya (nabhasaḥ) - tārakitam	'a starry sky'
20. yatta-debhyaḥ° *A*.5.2.39-41	yatparimāṇam asya-yāvat	'that which has specific measure'
21. saṁkhyāyāḥ° *A*.5.2.42	pañca avyavāḥ asya-pañcataya	'that which consists of five parts'
22. tadasmin-nadhika° *A*.5.2.45-47	ekādaśa adhikam asmin-ekādaśa (ekādaśam śatām)	'that in which there are eleven times more'
23. sa eṣām grāmaṇīḥ *A*.5.2.78	devadattaḥ gramaṇī reṣām te-devadatta-kaḥ	'villagers headed by Devadatta'
24. śṛṅkhala° *A*.5.2.79	śṛṅkhalam asya bandhanam śṛṅkhalakaḥ	'a young camel which is fettered or is tied with chains'
25. tadasmin-nannam° *A*.5.2.82-83	guḍāpūpaḥ prāyeṇa annam asyām-guḍā-pūpika (paurṇamāsī)	'a full-moon night wherein one generally takes a sweet baked food in loaf form made with jaggery'

26. śrāddhamanena° *A*.5.2.85	śrāddhamanena bhuktam-śrāddhikaḥ	'who has taken the food offered to the manes'
27. tadasyāstyasmin° *A*.5.2.94	gāvaḥ asya santi gomān	'possessing cows or cattle-wealth'

Lexical or Non-Syntactic Derivation

Little can be said about the *svārthika*-type of derivation excepting that the suffixes that fall under this group give some meaning to the bases to which they are added in certain cases. Further, the absence of any US precludes the possibility of the suffix conveying any *Kāraka*-relation too. Here the base for the suffixes is specified in TFR itself and most of the formations are lexically conditioned. As such when compared to the *asvārthika* type of derivation *svārthika* is less productive. Words like *devatā* which are of *svārthika* type do not signify any extra-sense than the sense of the base to which it is added. The word *devatā* for example, is derived from the stem *deva* by the addition of the suffix *taL* (*A*.5.4.27). It should be noted here that the suffix -*taL* is exclusively prescribed with reference to the stem *deva* and not to any other base. In this way such kind of suffixes are less productive than the other type of suffixes.[18]

Summary

Sanskrit word-formation has a unique feature in this that most of the complex words are derived from their underlying sentences. Sanskrit is highly poly-synthetic in nature, that is, it allows room for expressing complex sentences in a single word. Hence a complex word is related to its US. As stated above (Sec. 1.1) the syntactic relation is expressed explicitly through the complex words. In this regard, the TF is also one of the major devices to express the syntactic relation explicitly. A TS replaces all other linguistic expressions in an US except the one to which it is attached, that is the base. This shows that the word that is derived from the US is syntax-based. Viewed from the source of derivation, the TF is classified into two namely, Syntactic and Lexical Derivation. The *Taddhita* words that fall under the former group have the US-s as source and they also express the kāraka and non-kāraka relations. The *Taddhita* words that come under the purview of the latter group, however, merely add some senses; or, sometimes they modify the meaning of the base. The word that falls under the group of Lexical Derivation does not have any US and also does not convey any *kāraka*-relation.

In the following chapter we shall discuss the Semantic Features that are involved in the TF.

REFERENCES

1. In the case of *kṛt*-formation generally the US is not used to derive the new word. Only in the analytical level we notice an AS. For example, *kartā*. Herein the suffix *-tṛC* is added to the verbal root *kṛÑ* 'to do' to arrive the sense of an agent. The AS is *karoti yaḥ* - (kartā). Unlike the compounding and the TF the AS does not serve as the base.
2. A.2.1.26.
3. See Lyons, J., *Semantics*, Vol.II., pp. 534-50; Levi, *The Syntax and Semantics of Complex Nominals*; Bauer, L., *English Word-Formation*, Ch. III.
4. According to Pāṇini the compounding is of two types:
(i) that which belongs to non-*vibhāṣādhikāra* (that is, certain *avyayībhāva* compounds and *upapada* compounds).
(ii) that which belong to *vibhāṣādhikāra* like *tat-puruṣa*, etc. The present instance comes under the purview of the first type, namely, non-*vibhāṣādhikāra*. Here the *avyayībhāva*-compound is before the domain (rule) of *vibhāṣā* (A.2.1.1). Thus traditionally the *avyayībhāva*-compounds which come under this section, that is, non-*vibhāṣādhikāra* are characterised as *nitya samāsa* or obligatory compounding.
5. For detailed discussion on Restrictions on the WFR-s, See Bauer, L., *English Word-Formation*, pp. 84-100; Aronoff, M., *Word-Formation in Generative Grammar*, Ch. IV; Scalise, *Generative Morphology*, pp. 44-54; Jackendoff, *Morphological and Semantic Regularities in Lexicon*, p. 655.

6. See Sec. 1.7.3 in the present work.
7. Pāṇini's *Taddhita-Affixation Rules*, p. 16.
8 Misra, V.N., *The Descriptive Technique of Pāṇini*, p. 117.
9 *abhidhānam ca prāyena tiṄ-kṛttaddhita-samāsaiḥ*, *SK* on A.2.3.1.
10 Thus the rules *anabhihite* (A.2.3.1); *karmaṇi dvitīyā* (A.2.3.2); *kartṛkaraṇayotṛtīyā* (A.2.3.18); *caturthī sampradāne* (A.2.3.13); *apādāne pancamī* (A.2.3.28); *saptamyadhikarane ca* A.2.3.36 assign the appropriate case-endings to represent the above *Kāraka*-relations.
11. This is an instance of *upapadavibhakti*. Here the second case-ending is added to base by the rule *kālādhva* (A.2.3.5) to signify the sense of intimate connection.
12. Here the case-ending of the base is constituted from the preceding rule, namely, *tena raktam rāgād* (A.4.2.1). This is an example of *kartṛ-kāraka*-relation.
13. This is an example of *upapada vibhakti*.
14. *ibid.*
15. *ibid.*
16. Jesperson, O., *A Modern English Grammar*, Part VII, Syntax, pp. 306-341.
17. *ibid.*
18. See Aronoff, M., *Word-Formation in Generative Grammar*, Ch. III for details on productivity.

CHAPTER - V
SEMANTIC FEATURES INVOLVED IN TADDHITA-FORMATION

5.0. *Semantics and Word-Formation*

Semantics in Modern Linguistics has two main branches, namely, (1) Formal Semantics; and (2) Descriptive Semantics. Formal Semantics has its roots in philosophical logic and is closely allied to philosophy. However, most of the linguistic activity in the realm of Formal Semantics has been directed toward syntax, and not to morphology. Descriptive Semantics also known as Lexical Semantics under which the word-semantics is discussed is a pure linguistic enterprise started in the 19th century. Almost all descriptive semantists hold some version of the view of *lexical decomposition* according to which the meaning of a word can be broken into component parts. As noticed by Bauer[1] "There have been two main approaches to the problem of Word-Semantics. The first is illustrated by ordinary dictionaries of English, where word-meaning is specified in a number of ways including the listing of near synonyms ...... and the specification of function. The second is componential analysis in some form or other".[2] From this it can be said that the word in semantics has the function of conveying the meaning of a word through various factors.

Further just as the phonological feature of Word-Formation gives an appropriate pronunciation of the output, so also the semantic feature of Word-Formation takes care of the semantic reading with the help of its paraphrase. It is also known as semantic representation of the lexicon or output.[3] While deriving a new word out of an existing one, three process occur simultaneously:

1. morphological process [consisting in the change of the form of a word by the addition of a prefix or suffix];
2. syntactic process [consisting in the change of part of speech or the syntactic category of a base. Eg. V - N]; and
3. semantic process [giving rise to a new sense].

The following examples would make the above clear:

The Base	**Morphological process**	**Syntactic process**	**Semantic process**
laugh-laughter	involving addition of suffix-*ter*	change V - N	resultant form denoting an act or activity.
teach-teacher	involving addition of suffix-*er*	- do -	resultant form denoting an agent.
red-redness	involving addition suffix-*ness*	change Adj-N	resultant form denoting a property.

We shall now set forth the various features involved in Word-Formation Semantics.

1. The Word-Formation Semantics mostly deals with the semantic changes that take place in potential words, that is, words which are derived by the operation of regular WFRs. On the other hand, it pays very little attention to lexicalised words/forms. For example, the word *dāśarathiḥ* 'son of daśaratha'. Here the suffix - *iÑ* is added to the base *daśaratha(sya)* by the rule *ata iÑ* (*A*.4.1.95) to arrive at the sense of 'one's offspring'. The meaning of the new word is enjoined by the rule *tasyapatyam* which enables one to derive a large number of words. Similarly the word *sraughnaḥ* 'born in Srughna' is derived by the rule *tatra jātaḥ* (*A*.4.3.25) which is also a regular TFR. The semantics of WF mostly deals with these kinds of rules.

On the contrary words like *pītāṁbaraḥ*, etc., the meaning of which is lexicalised or restricted to a specific sense do not come within the range of WF semantics. Thus the WF semantics concentrates only on those words that are derived by the productive WFRs, and not on the words which have the idiomatic or idiosyncratic meanings. It is because, the words which carry idiomatic idiosyncratic meaning do not represent syncronic processes; rather they belong to a diachronic phenomenon and they are neither regular nor predictable.

2. Most of the potential words have a range of meanings rather than single meaning; and hence the task of WF semantics is to delimit this range, as stated by Bauer, L., "A recurrent problem in studies on Word-Formation is how closely the rules of Word-Formation should specify the meaning of a complex lexeme".[4] For example, the word *sraughnaḥ* has a wide range of meaning such as 'born in Srughna' - 'descendent of Srughna' - 'being/obtaining in Srughna' - 'arrived from Srughna' 'proceeds to Srughna' - 'arising from Srughna', 'residence of Srughna' - 'belongs to Srughna' etc. Here the WF Semantics delimits this range with the help of linguistic and non-linguistic context. As observed by Lyons, J.,[5] "....... the meaning of very complex lexemes is more specialised than that of the lexemes from which they appear to be derived. The reason for this would seem to be that complex lexemes are like simple lexemes ..... they may be institutionalized and by virtue of their use in particular context." Thus the meanings of newly derived words are normally determined from the meanings of their derivational components and from the context in which they are used.

3. Pragmatics plays a great role in the determination of the meanings of derived words. It may be defined in a wide sense as the influence of knowledge and beliefs about the structure of the real world, in contrast to knowledge about the language system. For instance, Jackendoff argues that "Part of a speaker's knowledge of the English lexicon is the way in which the meanings of compounds are related to the meanings of their constituents: thus we would say that somebody did not know English if he (seriously) used *garbage man* to mean a man made out of garbage by analogy with snowman".[6] The meaning of the compound form *garbage man* might seem odd, because the

meaning which is derived out of the word is not found in the real world, although it is not an ungrammatical one.[7]

4. One of the objectives of the WF semantics is to account for semantic relationships among the constituent members that occur in a derivation.

In short, each and every WFR has a more or less a significant impact upon the meaning of the base, and so a description of that change is given by the WF semantics.

We shall now discuss the role of semantics in the *Taddhita*-Formation.

5.1. *The Role of Semantics in Taddhita-Formation*

5.1.0. In the Pāṇinian system, the derivation of a word begins with Semantics and proceeds by introducing formative elements assigned with various meanings. The suffixes are thus introduced under meaning conditions and co-occurrence conditions. They are treated as signifier of specific meanings that are assigned to them in a given unit. The words derived by the addition of these suffixes are interchangeable with syntactic constructions or sentences on which they are based. For example, the sentence *vyākaraṇamadhīte* 'one who studies grammar' can be used in the place of its derivative or word - *vaiyākaraṇaḥ*. The point to be considered here is that the syntactic (*vyākaraṇam*) and morphological constructions (*vyākaraṇam* + - *aṆ*) though differ in structure and in their constituents, are acceptable equivalent to the ones in Sanskrit. In the above sentence, the constituents, namely, *vyākaraṇam* and *adhīte* are disparate entities; and *am* - the second case-ending in *vyākaraṇam* expresses the syntactic relation, namely, the *karmakāraka* relation in the present case. On the other hand, in the process of TF, the constituents *vyākaraṇa* and - *aṆ* form one unit but they do not have any syntactic relationship at the surface level. However, the two constituents belong to two different categories, namely, base and suffix. Pāṇini tries to link these categories with the help of meaning. It seems that Pāṇini should have proceeded on the assumption that *adhīte* in the above syntactic construction is equivalent semantically to the suffix - *aṆ*. It may optionally replace the syntactic item. When we opt for the latter, we have the string *vyākaraṇam - aṆ* instead of the sentence. Thus in the Pāṇinian derivational system there is an equation between constituents of a base structure which stands for the meaning and its output. And one of the constituents in the grammatical statements stands for the meaning of the suffix which the suffix replaces. The grammatical statements thus reflect the structure of underlying syntactic constructions on the one hand, and denote the meanings of the suffixes, on the other.

5.1.1. In the process of TF the nominal stems are generally found to be too many, while suffixes are few and finite. Pāṇini thus avoids the description of meanings of nominal bases. It is only rarely that he mentions the meaning of base and that too for the purposes of the specification of some words in specific senses. In such cases, the stem and suffixes are linked together through the meanings of the suffixes. Pāṇini thus takes meanings into consideration while initiating the process of word-derivation. In other words, the derivation has the semantic structure as the basis, and semantic structure is directly converted into surface structure by the processes that are laid down in the grammar.[8]

In the following sections we shall deal with the semantic conditions necessary for TF, semantically conditioned *taddhita*-suffixes, semantic classification of *taddhita*-suffixes and also various semantic domains *arthādhikāra*-s found in TF.

5.2. Let us begin with the discussion on the semantic condition essential for TF.

5.2.0. Pāṇini's grammatical rules concerning *padavidhi* are exclusively related to semantically connected (*samartha*) elements. That is to say, the aphorism-*samarthaḥ padavidhiḥ* (*A*.2.1.1) puts a semantic condition on the base in the process of Word-formation. In the process of deriving a new word from the existing base the latter must have semantic fitness or appropriateness to its constituent member. This is the pre-requisite in the process of any Word-formation.[9] For example, the expression *rājapuruṣaḥ* - 'king's servant'. Herein the constituent member of the US namely, *rājñaḥ puruṣaḥ* are semantically congruous with each other; and hence we have the compound word *rājapuruṣaḥ*. In the contrary instances such as *bhāryā rājñaḥ puruṣo devadattasya* 'the wife of the king, the servant of Devadatta', the words 'of the king' and 'servant' cannot be compounded with each other, since they are not semantically congruous. If, however, they are compounded, we would have the incorrect form — **bhāryā rājapuruṣo devadattasya*. Thus *sāmarthya* or semantic compatibility is a basic requirement for the constituent members so that they may be harmoniously blended together resulting in a new correct form.

5.2.1. In regard to the TF also the above said condition is essential. The rule *samarthānām prathamād vā* (*A*.4.1.82) stipulates that the *taddhita*-suffixes are applied optionally to the first of the semantically related constituent members specified in each rule. For example, *aupagavaḥ* 'a descendent of *upagu*'. Here the constituents of the US, namely *upagoḥ* and *apatyam* are semantically compatible with each other. Thus by the rule *tasyāpatyam* (*A*.4.1.92), we derive the word *aupagavaḥ*. It must be added here that semantic compatibility is a general condition for the derivation of all types of Word-formation.

5.2.2. Besides the general condition of semantic compatibility, we notice that there are two more specific conditions in regard to TFR-s/suffixes one relating to the base and the other, to the output.

5.2.2.1. In regard to the former, we shall cite illustrative examples now:

1. The suffix - *cha* is added to the words signifying a mountain (*parvata*) as in the case of *hṛdgolīyaḥ* 'mercenaries whose ancestral home is Hṛdgola'.

2. The suffix - *ḍhaÑ* (*A*.4.1.135) is added to the words signifying quadrupeds (*catuṣpādbhyaḥ*) as in the case of *kamaṇḍaleyaḥ*, etc.

3. The suffix - *ṭhaÑ* (*A*.4.2.47) is added to the words denoting inanimate objects (*acitta*) and the words *hasti*

'elephant' and *dhenu* 'cow' to convey the sense of multitude as in the case of *āpūpikaḥ* 'a collection of cakes', etc.

4. The suffix - *ṭhaÑ* (*A*.4.3.68) is added to the words consisting of names of Vedic sacrifices (*kratu*) and domestic sacrifices (*yajñebhyaḥ*) as in the case of *āgniṣṭomikaḥ* 'a ommentary on *Agniṣṭoma*'.

5. The suffix - *ṭhaK* (*A*.4.3.96) is added to the words denoting an inanimate thing (*accitta*) other than those representing locality or time (*adeśakala*) as in the case of *āpūpikaḥ* 'person fond of cakes'. If the base denotes either an animate being or location or time, the above suffix - *ṭhaK* does not take place. Instead the suffix - *aṆ* (*A*.4.1.83) is added to the bases as in the case of *daivadattaḥ, sraughnaḥ* and *graiṣmaḥ* respectively.

6. The suffix - *yaT* (*A*.4.3.55) is added to the bases that signify a member of body (*śarīrāvayava*) as in the case of *dantyam* 'dental' related to the teeth, *dante bhavam*. The same suffix with the similar base is also used to denote the sense of 'good or beneficial for it'. For example, *dentebhyaḥ hitam* = *dantyam* 'beneficial to the teeth' (*A*.5.1.6). It should be noted here that though the morphological form of the base (*danta* + *yaT*) as well as the output (*dantyam*) are the same in the both the cases, yet, there is a difference between the two. The former one which is derived out of the US, namely, *dante bhavam* is an exception to the general suffix - *aṆ*. That is, the suffix - *yaT* supersedes the - *aṆ* in the case of the bases denoting member of body to arrive at the sense of *tatra bhavaḥ* 'occurred therein'. The latter one which is derived out of the US, namely, *dantebhyaḥ hitam* is an exception to the general suffix - *cha*. Herein the suffix - *yaT* supersedes the - *cha* in the cases of the bases designating a member of body to arrive at the sense of *tasmai hitam* (*A*.5.1.6). From the above it emerges that though the base and the resultant form resemble each other, yet there is a difference in their US-s which represent the meanings of the outputs.

7. The suffix - *kaN* (*A*.5.1.22) is added to the words denoting numerical words excluding those ending in - *ti* and

- *śat* as in the case of *pañcakaḥ* 'bought with five pieces'. (*pañcabhyaḥ kritaḥ*). Here the numerical base does not end with - *ti* or *śat*. Hence the suffix - *kaN* is added. This is an exception to the general suffix - *thaÑ*. On the contrary, for the numerical bases ending with the suffix - *ti*, and - *śat* the general suffix - *ṭhaÑ* is added as in the cases of *saptatyā krītaḥ* = *sāptatikaḥ* 'bought with seventy' and *caturviṁśatyā krītaḥ* = *cāturviṁśatikaḥ* 'bought with twenty-four'.

Exactly similar consideration applies to the case of *pañcakaḥ* 'the five (birds)' (*A*.5.1.58). Here the suffix - *kaN* is added to the words denoting numerical words.

Similar treatment is noticed even in cases outside the TF. Thus in compounding *vibhāṣāvṛkṣamṛga*° (*A*.2.4.12) the individual words *aśva, vadava pūrva*, etc., are classed along with the words denoting *vṛkṣa* 'trees', *mṛga* 'animals', *tṛṇa* 'grasses', etc., to form the *dvandva* compounds optionally. For example, *plakṣanyagrodham/plakṣanyagrodhāḥ* '*plakṣa* and *Nyagrodha* trees', *rurupṛṣatam/ruru pṛṣatāḥ* '*ruru* and antelopes', etc. Thus the semantic condition is not exclusive to the TF; rather it a general one in the process of Word-Formation.

So far the discussion regarding the semantic requirement for the base. Now we shall discuss the semantic requirement for the output.

5.2.3.2. *The Semantic Criterion for the Output*

In the case of the output, it may refer to a particular object, an activity or a person or even a particular class of objects or persons (*samjñā*). It may be noted that on the basis of the semantic criteria, namely, the semantic specifications of the output only the suffixes are enjoined to their respective bases. Thus in the following case we notice certain suffixes that are specified by semantic criterion of the output.

1. The suffix - *yaÑ* (*A*.4.1.106-108) is added to the words *madhu* and *babhru* when the words so formed mean 'a Brahmin' and 'the one who comes in the line of *kauśika*' respectively as in the case of *mādhavyaḥ* = *brahmaṇaḥ* and *bābhravyaḥ* = *kauśikaḥ*. In other cases the suffix - *aṆ* is added as in the case of *mādhavaḥ* and *bābhravaḥ*.

2. The suffix - *ḍhaK* - *eya* (*A*.4.1.124) is added to the words *vikarṇa* and *kuṣitaka* when the words so formed mean the descendants of *kāśyapa* as in the case of *vaikarṇeyaḥ* and *kauṣītakeyaḥ* = *kāśyapaḥ*; otherwise we would have *vaikarṇiḥ* and *kauṣatakiḥ* formed by *A*.4.1.95.

3. The suffix - *vyaN* (*A*.4.1.145) is added to the word *bhrātṛ* when the word so formed means 'an enemy' as in the case of *bhrātṛvyaḥ* = *sapatnaḥ* 'an enemy'. Otherwise we would have *bhrātrīyaḥ* and *bhrātṛvyaḥ* formed by *A*.4.1.143 and 144.

4. The suffix - *Ṇa* (*A*.4.1.147-49) is added after a feminine word denoting a *gotra* - descendent when the words so formed mean 'contempt' as in the case of *gārgaḥ* = *jālmaḥ*.

5. The suffixes - *aÑ* and - *yaT* (*A*.4.1.161) are added to the word *manu* and also the augment *ṣUK* is added when these suffixes follow, provided that the word so formed denotes a class name *jāti* as in the case of *mānuṣaḥ* and *manuṣyaḥ* 'a man or a man-kind'. When the descendent is to be expressed the suffix -*aṆ* is added as in the case of *māṇavaḥ* 'son of Manu'.

6. The suffix - *matUP* (*A*.4.2.58) is added to the bases such as *udumbara, maśaka*, etc., when the words so formed denotes a name of a river as in the case of *udumbarāvati*. Otherwise, we would have *audumbaraḥ* formed by *A*.4.1.83.

7. The suffix - *ḍhakaÑ* (*A*.4.2.96) is added to the words *kula, kukṣi, grīvā*, when the words so formed mean 'a dog', 'a sword', and 'an ornament' respectively as in the case of *kauleyakaḥ* 'a dog', *raukṣeyakaḥ* 'a sword' and *graiveyakaḥ* 'a necklace'. In other cases, the suffix - *aṆ* is added as in the cases of *kaulaḥ,raukṣaḥ* and *graivaḥ*.

8. The suffixes - *ṢphaK* and - *aṆ* (*A*.4.2.100) are added, to the word *raṅku* when the word so formed means 'a non-human being' (*amanuṣya*) as in the case of *rāṅkavāyaṇaḥ, rāṅkavaḥ* = *gauḥ* 'a cow'. Otherwise we would have *rāṅkavakaḥ* = *manuṣyaḥ* 'a man' formed by *A*.4.2.134.

9. The suffix - *VuÑ* (*A*.4.2.129) is added to the word *araṇya*, when the word so formed means 'a man' *manuṣya* as in the case of *āraṇyakaḥ* = *manuṣyaḥ* 'a man' (a forester). Otherwise we would have *āraṇyāḥ paśavaḥ* 'wild beasts' formed by *A*.4.1.83.

10. The suffix - *VuÑ* (*A*.4.2.128) is added to the word *nagara*, when the word so formed means 'censure or praise' as in the case of *nāgarakaḥ* 'a knave, a cunning person, or a skillful person'. Otherwise we would have *nāgārāḥ* = *bhrāhmaṇāḥ* 'the Nagara Brahmanas' formed by *A*.4.1.82.

11. The suffix - *VuÑ* (*A*.4.2.134) is added to the words such as *kaccha, sindhu*, etc. when the words so formed mean 'a man' or 'What exists in man' as in the case of *kacchakaḥ* 'a man born in Kutch'. Otherwise we would have *kaccho gauḥ* 'The cow of Kutch' formed by *A*.4.1.83.

12. The suffix - *cha* (*A*.4.2.144) is added optionally to the word *parvata* when the word so formed does not denote a man as in the cases of *pārvatīyāni* or *pārvātāni phalāni* 'hill fruits'. Otherwise we would have *parvatīyo manuṣyaḥ* 'the hill man' formed by *A*.4.2.143, where no option is allowed.

13. The suffix - *ṭhaÑ* (*A*.4.3.12) is added to the word *śarada* when the word so formed means 'a funeral oblation' as in the case of *śāradikaḥ* 'the autumnal śrāddha'. Otherwise it will be *śāradam* 'born in autumn season' formed by *A*.4.1.83.

14. The suffix - *ṭhaÑ* (*A*.4.3.13) is added optionally to the word *śarada* when the word so formed means 'illness or heat' as in the case of *śāradiko rogaḥ*, 'the autumnal disease'. Otherwise we would have *śāradam dadhi* 'the autumnal curd' formed by *A*.4.1.83.

15. The suffix - *ṭhaÑ* (*A*.4.3.69) is added to the words denoting a *ṛṣhi*, when the word so formed means 'an adhyāya or chapter' of a work as in the case of *vāsiṣṭhiko' dhyāyaḥ* 'a chapter containing commentary on Vāsiṣṭha'. Otherwise we would have *vāsiṣṭhī ṛk* formed by *A*.4.1.83.

16. The suffix - *Nini* (*A*.4.3.105) is added to the words such as *śāṭyāyana*, etc., when the word so formed denotes 'a Brahmaṇa' or 'a Kalpa-work enounced by ancient sages' as in the case of *śāṭyāyanīnaḥ* 'a Brahmaṇa work of Śāṭyāyana'.

17. The suffix - *Ṇini* (*A*.4.3.110) is added to the words *pārāśarya* and *śilalin* when the words so formed denote *Bhikṣu - sūtra* and *Naṭa-sūtra* respectively as in the cases of *pārāśarī* 'the

treatise of *pārāśarya* on the duties of Bhikṣus'. Otherwise we would have the word *pāraśaram, śailālam* formed by *A*.4.1.83.

18. The suffix - *yaT* is added to the words such as *pāda, ūrū,* etc., provided that 'it is not a bow', with which anything is pierced' as in the case of *padyāḥ śarkarāḥ* 'what pierce the feet' that is, 'pebbles'. Otherwise no suffix is added as in the case of *pādau vidhyati dhanuṣā.*

Apart from the exceptional cases even in the regular process also there are some bases as well as the output specified semantically. As noticed[10] by Joshi, D.M., "in some cases the meanings for which affixes are introduced are qualified by other meanings. That is, the items which are called AS are qualified by other items whose meanings qualify the meanings of the AS. The affix then is introduced to express the qualified meaning". For example, *puṣyeṇa yuktāḥ māsaḥ* = *pauṣam,* 'the month connected with *puṣya*'. Here the word *puṣya* denoting a constellation (*nakṣtra vācī*) denotes also a month (*māsa*). The base is qualified by the meaning 'month' (*māsa*). In other words, the word designating a constellation and also denoting a month acts as a base for the present derivation. Similarly the meaning of the output, namely, *yuktaḥ* 'connected' is qualified by the meaning of time (*kāla*). That is, the output denotes the meaning of connection as well as time. Thus in the present case, the base as well as the output are specified semantically. This may be characterised as *padaviśeṣaṇa* and *arthaviśeṣaṇa* where the former one relates to the semantic specification of a base and the latter to the output. The distinction between other types of regular process on the one hand, and the present one on the other is that in other cases the base as well as the output are not viewed in relation to any semantic criterion. In the cases of *tasyāpatyam* (*A*.4.1.92) *tasyedam* (*A*.4.3.120) etc., one can take any genitive-ending *pada* as a base. For example, *aupagavaḥ dāśarathiḥ,* etc. Here the bases are *upagu* and *daśaratha* to which the suffixes - *aṆ* and *iÑ* are added respectively. The meanings of the outputs may be either of the following namely, descendent of *upagu,* the one which belongs to *upagu* and descendent of Daśaratha the one which belongs to Daśaratha respectively. In the above cases there is no semantic specification of the base or output excepting the injunction of meaning to the suffix.

As already stated above the semantic specification of the base occurs in other cases like compounding. In the case of the latter the output, that is, the compound word may refer to either a particular object, or activity or person or even a particular class of objects or persons.[11] Thus, the word *unmattagaṅgam* which is an *avyayībhāva*-compound refers to a particular country, namely, the city of Varanasi. Similarly, the compound words such as *khaṭvārūdhaḥ* 'one who is recklessly audacious' etc., which are lexicalised forms come under this type.

In the case of words in feminine gender, there are some feminine suffixes which could be added only when the output denotes a particular person or object which is different from the one that is conveyed by the word in regular process. For example, the feminine formative *ṬāP* is added to the stem when the output refers to a Vedic hymn, as in the case *dvipadā ṛk* 'a *ṛk* with two lines'.[12] In contrast to the above, it may be pointed out that when the output refers to senses other than the specified one, the suffix - *ṄīP* is added as in the case of *dvipadī devadattaḥ* 'Devadatta is two-legged'. It emerges from the above discussion that Pāṇini may be taken to have followed the method of semantic specification of the base as well as the output. In this way the process of TF also involves some similar types of suffixes.

5.3. *Endo-centric and Exo-centric Constructions*

5.3.0. *Taddhita* constructions (Formation) can be classified into two groups according to the semantic criteria, namely, (1) endocentric; and (2) exocentric.

5.3.0.1. *Endocentric Constructions*

A construction involving the meaning of its constituent member is termed endocentric construction. In other words, the construction exclusively refers to the meaning of the constituents. For example, the word *āḍhyatama* 'richest' which is derived from the base *āḍhya* by the addition of the suffix *tamaP* (A.5.3.52) refers to a modified sense of the base namely, *atiśayena āḍhyaḥ āḍhyatamaḥ*, 'richest'. That is, the suffix *tamaP* merely modifies the meaning of the base and thus, the output refers to one and the same sense with slight change in the base conveyed by the base.

5.3.0.2. *Exocentric Constructions*

Any construction which is not an endocentric is exocentric.[13] It would have reference to something that is other than the meanings of the constituent members. For example, the word *vaiyākaraṇaḥ* refers to a grammarian which is not the meaning of either of the constituents, namely, *vyākaraṇa* and *adhīte*. Here the suffix - *aṆ* (A.4.2.83) is added to the base *vyākāraṇa* to bring out the sense of 'one who studies' or knows and the US is represented as *vyākaraṇam adhīte*. Thus in such cases the output refers to a third member, other than the meanings of the constituents of the constructions.

5.3.0.3. In regard to TF the constructions which are formed with *svārthika* type of suffixes may be brought under the endocentric construction. In this case, the suffixes do not change the meaning of the base completely, rather they slightly modify it. Thus the output refers a modified sense of the base.[14]

5.3.0.4. The construction which is formed out of the addition of *asvārthika* type of suffixes, however, falls under the purview of the exocentric construction whose meaning is different from that of the constituent members.

5.3.1. *The Semantic Classification of Taddhita-Suffixes*

5.3.1.0. The *Taddhita*-suffixes when considered in relation to their semantic features may be classified into *asvārthika*-s or *vācaka*-s and *svārthika*-s or *dyotakas*. Pāṇini in his *Aṣṭādhyāyi* has not classified so, but his commentators have brought out such a classification.

5.3.1.1. *Asvārthika*-s or *Vācaka*-s

The *asvārthika*-suffixes are those that denote some meanings which are not expressed by the base to which they are added. Thus they are prescribed to denote a special meaning. This meaning is represented by a paraphrase (*vigraha vākya*) from which the word is derived. For example, the suffix - *aṆ* when this suffix is added to the base *upagu*, it conveys the meaning of the son of *upagu* (*upagorapatyam*) which is different from the meaning of base *upagu*. Hence these are termed as *asvārthika* suffixes.

5.3.1.2. The *asvārthika*-suffixes are largest in number followed by *svārthika*-s. These can further be classified into two groups. The first group comprising of suffixes which are prescribed along with their meanings; and the second one comprising of suffixes which are not enjoined along with their meanings. We shall take the first group first for discussion.

In the case of the first group of suffixes the latter such as *aṆ*, *ṭhaK*, etc., are enjoined along with exceptions. This process of classification is known as *pratyayādhikāra*. The *pratyayādhikāra* is classified on the basis of various general suffixes and the upper limit of their application is specified with the meanings. For example, the general suffix - *aṆ* is enjoined to denote a variety of meanings that are stated upto the rule *tena divyati khanati jayati jitam* (A.4.4.2). There are nearly fifty types of meanings stated in this domain. Further, some suffixes under this group convey an identical sense. The unit comprising of such suffixes is known as falling under the category of *arthādhikāra*. The point that is of importance here is that the *arthādhikāra* is a constituent of *pratyayādhikāra*. It is only the *asvārthika*-type of suffixes that can be classified into various *pratyayādhikāra*-s and *arthādhikāra*-s. It is because, these two are always connected with the denotative power of the suffixes. As has been pointed out earlier, these suffixes are enjoined always with their meanings. For example, the suffix - *aṆ* is an *asvārthika* type of suffix. This is enjoined to denote various senses such as *tasyāpatyam* (*A*.4.1.92); *tenaraktam rāgāt*; (*A*.4.2.1) etc. Under each and every meaning heading there are several exceptions such as *ata iÑ* (*A*.4.1.95); *lākṣā rocanātthaK* (*A*.4.2.2) etc., for specific bases or environments. Thus any suffix that is enjoined along with its meaning would come under this category.

5.3.1.3. There are some *asvārthika* type of suffixes which are not enjoined along with their meanings. In regard to these, the sufixes are enumerated along with the specific bases/ environments first, and then, the meanings are assigned to the suffixes. It should be noted here that the second type of *asvārthika* suffixes does not convey a single meaning; rather it denotes a variety of senses (See Sec. 3.). For example, the suffixes enumerated in *A*.4.2.92-4.3.24) which come under the purview of *śeṣe* (*A*.4.2.92). Here the so-called *śaiṣika*-suffixes denote all the senses that are listed in *A*.4.3.25-4.3.120. A similar type of enumeration of suffixes is noticed in the case of suffixes listed in *A*.5.1.18-36 which denote all the senses that are stated in *A*.5.1.37-63.

5.3.1.4. The enumeration of suffixes at one place and the specification of the meanings elsewhere are found in the *kṛt*-formation also. In the *kṛt*-formation there is an enumeration of a large number of suffixes alongwith the exceptions for the specific bases/environments first. And at the end of the *kṛt*-section Pāṇini states the actual meanings of the *kṛt* suffixes in the aphorisms *kartari kṛt* (*A*.3.4.67), *tayoreva kṛtya kta khalarthāḥ* (*A*.3.4.70) etc. It may be added here that there are some *kṛt* suffixes such as *ghaÑ*, *LyuT*, etc., enjoined in the rules *akartari ca kārake saṁjñāyām* (*A*.3.3.19); *kṛtya LyuṬo bahulam* (3.3.113) to denote some specific senses, namely 'a *kāraka* other than the agent (*akartari*) when the output refers to a proper name (*saṁjñāyām*)', etc. But, normally, the meaning of the *kṛt* suffix is stated at the end of the *kṛt* section; that is, after the enumeration of the *kṛt* suffixes. From the above it is presumed that Pāṇini would have followed the similar pattern in regard to the second type of *asvārthika*-suffixes.

5.3.1.5. As already stated above, the *asvārthika* suffixes denote a special meaning other than the sense of the base. In other words, these suffixes have the denotative capacity. In this regard these can be further grouped into different *arthādhikāra*-s.[14] It should be borne in mind that the major part of the *taddhita*-suffixes belongs to the *asvārthika* type. This two-fold classification of suffixes as falling under the *pratyayādhikāra* and the *arthādhikāra* has relevance to the *asvārthika* type of suffixes only. In the case of the *svārthika* type of suffixes too we find some suffixes coming under the purview of *pratyayādhikāra*, namely, *ka* in the rule *prāgivātkaḥ* (*A*.5.3.70). But the suffix *ka* is enjoined in such a way that it does not change the meaning of the base in full; rather, it is meant merely to indicate the specific sense in which a word has been used. Similarly *asvārthika* type of suffixes is more productive than the *svārthika*-s which are enjoined for specific bases only. Further, the *asvārthika* type of suffixes expresses the *kāraka* relations through their US-s, whereas *svārthika* type is not so. In short, *asvārthika* type of suffixes covers the major part of the TF.

5.3.2. *Svārthika*-s or *Dyotaka*-s

The *svārthika* type of suffixes does not denote any special meaning other than the modification of the meaning of the base (*svīye prakṛtyarthe bhavāḥ svārthikāḥ* 'refers to one's own base-meaning'). These are enumerated in the last two sections of the Fifth Chapter of the *Aṣṭādhyāyī*. It is defined as a suffix which is meant merely to indicate the specific sense in which a word is used.[15] In other words, it is simply indicative of the meaning of the bases.[16] For example, the suffixes *tamaP* and *iṣṭhaN* (*A*.5.3.55) are added to the bases, namely, '*āḍhya*' and *paṭu* respectively. The resultant form is *āḍhyatama* 'richest' and *paṭiṣṭhaḥ* 'most skilled'. Here the suffixes merely indicate that the bases *āḍhya* and *paṭu* are used in the sense of 'superlative excellence (*atśāyane*)' that is, *atiśayena āḍhyaḥ* = *āḍhyatamaḥ* and *atiśayena patuḥ*. Thus the function of a *svārthika* suffix is comparable to that of a lamp which brings to the notice of a person an object that is already existing. It may be added here that in most of the cases the *svārthika* type of suffixes is added to the bases obligatorily.[17] The commentary - *kāśika* on the rule *A*.4.1.82 restricts the scope of the recurrence of the rule upto the *asvārthikā* - type of suffixes only in view of the fact that under the jurisdiction of *svārthika*-s the recurrence of the above rule *A*.4.1.82 is not fully effective. To quote ...... *svārthikeṣu hyasya upayogo nāsti, vikalpopi tatrānavasthitaḥ; kecinnityameva bhavanti.*[18]

A close study of the *svārthika*-suffixes has led the commentators on the *Aṣṭādhyāyi* to classify them into *svārthika*-s and *atyanta-svārthika*-s. As stated above the svārthika suffixes are indicative of some specific feature already existent in the meaning of the bases. But, the *atyanta svārthika*-s do not serve the purpose. For example, the suffixes - *ka* and - *kaN* which are added to the bases *avi* 'sheep' and to the words in the group that begins with *yāva*[19] 'made of barley'. The resultant forms such as *avikaḥ* and *yāvakaḥ* are synonymous with the bases to which they are added. In such cases we do not find any addition of meaning to the bases. As noticed by Cardona, G.,"There are also affixes for which meanings are not explicitly stated (*anirdiṣṭārthāḥ*) in Pāṇinian sūtra-s. Pāṇinians from Kātyāyana onwords invoke a meta-rule, not formulated in the *Aṣṭādhyāyī* according to which such affix occurs redundantly in meanings proper to elements with which they are used. Although such affixes do not have meanings which they alone signify, they are nevertheless not considered meaningless, instead, they are treated as reduntantly meaningful in that meanings attributed to them are said to be signified properly by other elements. Pāṇiniyas refer to these as *svārthikāḥ pratyayāḥ* 'affixes with redundant meanings'. In addition, they distinguish between affixes qualified simply as *svārthika*-s and others, which are said to be absolutely redundant (*atyanta svārthika*-s)".[20]

The difference between these two kinds of suffixes is that the former indicates the sense of the base while the latter do not. Besides, the former differ from the latter in regard to the character of their bases. That is, *svārthika*-s are added to a nominal ending (word) (*subanta*) and the *atyanta svārthika*-s, to a nominal stem (*prātipadika*).[21]

The suffixes that are added to compounds are widely known as *samasānta*. These are enumerated under the heading *samāsāntāḥ* (*A*.5.4.68) a subsection of rules which prescribes *taddhita* suffixes. This group of suffixes is also considered as *atyanta svārthika*-s. For example, the suffix *ṬaC* (*A*.5.4.91) is added to the compound stems - *rājan, ahan* and - *sakhi*. The segments - *an* in *rāj*(*an*) and *ah(an)* and - *i* in - *sakh(i)* are deleted before the addition of the *taddhita*-suffix by the rules *nastaddhite* (*A*.6.4.144) and *yasyeti ca* (*A*.6.4.148) respectively. (See Sec 2.4.2.2). By this deletion, the rule which enjoins the suffix *ṬaC* serves to derive compounds with - *rāja, āha* and - *sakha*. Thus the compound forms such as *paramarājaḥ, paramasakhaḥ* are derived from the underlying sentences *paramo rājā* and *paramo sakhā* respectively. In these cases, by the addition of the suffix *ṬaC* there is no addition of meaning to the constituent members, namely, *parama* or *rājan* or *sākhi* except the phonological changes. Thus the *samāsānta* suffixes neither signify nor indicate any particular meaning and so they are treated as *atyanta svārthika*-s.

5.4. *Various Meaning-Adhikāra*-s *Found in TF*

5.4.0. *The Nature and the Scope of the Meaning Adhikāra*-s *in TF*

In the *taddhita* section of the *Aṣṭādhyāyī* each meaning of the derivatives is stated in the form of a phrase containing more than one constituent. Of these, the first constituent member of the phrase or the US acts as a base for the derivation.[22] The remaining constituent(s) actually stand(s) for the meaning or the semantic representation of the output. For example, the rule *tasyāpatyam* (*A*.4.1.92) which enjoins the meaning for the given suffixes in the form of a phrase contains two constituents namely, *tasya* and *apatyam*. The former one signifies the base of the derivation, that is, a genitive case-ending word which is semantically compatible with other item. The latter one gives the appropriate semantic reading of the output. Thus the rules which are stated to denote the meaning of the output in the form of phrases contain a base with a different case-ending and an item which refers to the meaning. In the above case, the words *tasya* and *apatyam* represent the base as well as the meaning respectively. However in some cases we find some of the meaning-statements in the form of finite verbal ending as in the cases of *tarati* (*A*.4.4.5), *carati* (*A*.4.4.8), etc. In these cases the base recurs from the previous rule with a specified case-ending. In the above instances, the instrumental case-ending word recurs from the previous rule, namely, *tena dīvyati* .... (*A*.4.4.2). As stated[23] above one of the functions of the WFR is to specify the base for the derivation alongwith the semantic reading of the output. We find similar pattern in Pāṇini's TF also. Here for each and every suffix, Pāṇini prescribes the base, alongwith its meaning. Thus in the *Taddhita* section, the meaning-statements not only signify the meanings, but also aid the bases for derivation.

5.4.1. Earlier it has been said that the *asvārthika*-type of suffixes has the denotative power to express various senses that are assigned under several meaning-headings. The meanings of the suffix as well as the output are represented through the underlying sentences (phrases) or the *vigraha vākya*-s which are the sources of derivation (See Sec. 4.2). Each and every US (meaning-heading) governs a number of suffixes. In other words, the same meaning is expressed by a variety of suffixes.[24] For example the *apatyādhikāra* (*A*.4.1.92-178). This consists of nearly twenty five suffixes, for denoting the single sense of 'an offspring'. Hence this *adhikāra* is known as *arthādhikāra*. In regard to the TF, Pāṇini has specified nearly one hundred and seventy five meaning-headings which stand for an *adhikāra*. That is, each and every meaning-heading is treated as a meaning *adhikāra*. This has been explained by Bhate thus: "Each one of the *arthādhikāra* further contains a number of rules reaching different suffixes to specific stems. With the exception of a few cases this arangement goes smooth throughout the *taddhita*-section".[25] The *arthādhikāra* is identified on the basis of the general statements found in this section. Thus each meaning bearing statement or phrase has a wide range of application covering a variety of suffixes. In short, a meaning bearing statement is an *adhikāra*. For example, *tasyāpatyam* (*A*.4.1.92), *tena raktam rāgāt* (*A*.4.2.1) etc. These two *adhikāra*-s contain within themselves manifold suffixes fit to be applied to specified bases.

5.4.2. The longest and the most important of all the *arthādhikāra*-s is the *apatyādhikāra*. The rule *tasyā patyam* (*A*.4.1.92) which prescribes the meaning of progeny governs nearly twenty five varieties of suffixes. Of these, the suffix - *aṆ* is a major one which is prescribed in a general manner. That is, the suffix - *aṆ* (*A*.4.1.83) is enjoined without making any condition on it (See Sec. 3.1). The remaining suffixes such as *iÑ* (*A*.4.1.95), *phaK* (*A*.4.1.99), *yaÑ* (*A*.4.1.105), etc., are exceptions to the - *aṆ* in a specific environment.

5.4.3. Following the *apatyādhikāra* there are various meaning *adhikāra*-s such as *raktādyarthaka, cāturarthika, śaiṣika,* etc. Here the *raktādyārthaka* contains a number of meaning headings in which each heading governs some suffixes. For example, the rule *tadadhite tadveda* (*A*.4.2.59) which prescribes a meaning *adhikāra* governing five suffixes. It should be borne in mind that in all these meaning - *adhikāra*-s, the suffix, namely, - *aṆ* which is enjoined in a general manner is added. In other words, unless otherwise a suffix is specified for a specific base/ environment the suffix - *aṆ* is added generally. It may be added here that an *arthādhikāra* usually contains a single meaning which is followed in all the specified rules. But in the case of *cāturarthika* there are four meanings namely, *tadasminnastiti deśe* (*A*.4.2.67), *tena nirvṛttam* (*A*.4.2.68), *tasya nivasaḥ,* (*A*.4.2.69), *adūra bhavaśca* (*A*.4.2.70) prescribed simultaneously and the suffixes are enjoined with a view to convey these meanings. The suffixes prescribed under this *adhikāra* would be applicable to anyone or even more than one of the meanings stated above.

5.4.4. As stated above[26] the second type of *asvārthika*-suffixes is enumerated in a different manner. In the case of *śaiṣika* suffixes Pāṇini enumerates some suffixes first and then, he prescribes some meaning-headings. These meaning-headings, however, govern some suffixes that are enumerated preceding the meaning-stating rules, and also some suffixes that are specified under each and every meaning headings.[27] It should be noted here that a meaning-*adhikāra* generally would govern some suffixes that are specified after the meaning headings. But in the cases of the suffixes that are enumerated in the *śaiṣika* section under the heading *śeṣa* (*A*.4.2.92) and the suffixes enjoined in the First Chapter of Fifth *adhyāya* we find the arrangement of meaning-headings in a different manner. Like the *cāturarthika* type of suffixes, in the present case also the suffixes prescribed under this *adhikāra* would express any one of the meanings listed in this section or even more than one of the meanings stated along with that. For example, the word *sraughnaḥ* which is derived from the base *srughna* by the addition of the suffix - *aṆ* would express any one of these senses; namely, 'born there', 'coming from there', 'belongs to him', etc. The method adopted by Pāṇini in prescribing suffixes with reference to some senses in the meaning - *adhikāra* of the *śaiṣika*-section is quite different from the one adopted in other sections of the *Taddhita*.

5.4.5. Like the *apatyādhikāra*, the *matvarthīya* section of the TF is also one of the lengthy meaning - *adhikāra* which governs nearly thirty suffixes to denote the sense of 'whose it is' (*tadasyāsti*) or 'in whom it is' (*tadasminnasti*). In other words, the suffix-*matUP* is added to bring out the senses of 'one who possesses that' or 'which contains it'. This is also widely known as possessive suffixes which are traditionally known as *matvarthīyapratyaya*. The different types of suffixes which are enumerated in this section are exceptions to the suffix - *matUP* that is prescribed in a general manner. The remaining suffixes are specified for specific bases. The limitations of the meanings of suffixes enjoined in the sense of - *matUP* have been summed up by Patañjali, in a metrical form thus:

bhūminindā praśaṁsāyām nityayoge'tiśayane
saṁsarge'sti vivakṣayām bhavanti matupādayaḥ.[28]

The suffix-*matUP* and the suffixes that are enjoined alongwith this are added to bring out the following senses.

1. a large quantity or number as in *gomān* 'having many cows';
2. when censure is implied as in *kakudāvarthi* 'hump, backed', *samkhadaki* 'foothed', 'fanged';
3. when praise is meant, as in *rūpavati kanyā;*
4. when an inherent or permanent quality of a thing is to be indicated as in *kṣiriṇo vṛkṣāḥ;*
5. when excellence is meant, as in *udariṇī kanyā;*
6. when accompaniment is implied as in *daṇḍī, chatrī;* and
7. when the sense of *asti* 'to be' is denoted as in *astimān.*

Thus the *matvarthīya* is one of the important meaning *adhikāra*-s in the *Taddhita* section.

5.4.6. So far as the meaning headings in regard to the *Taddhita*-section are concerned, Pāṇini has stated the meanings of the suffixes in the majority of cases. That is, he has considered many important types of meanings usually expressed by the speakers of the language, by the application of the TS-s. Even after this one might say that these meanings are merely indications (*upalakṣaṇa*) of a particular shade of meaning. The other shades of meaning must be taken as understood; they may be expressed by the same suffix too. It is usually claimed that words and their meanings are not taught by Grammar. But in so far as the *taddhita* words and their meanings are concerned, we find they are derived by the application of the grammatical rules.

Summary

In this chapter we have discussed the semantic features that are involved in TF. In this regard we have given the role of semantics in Word-Formation in general and the TF in particular. Further, we have analysed the semantically conditioned TS-s. We noticed two types semantic criterion, one related to the base and the other related to the output in regard to the application of certain TS-s. The TS-s are classified into *asvārthika*-s and *svārthika*-s on the basis of the denotative power of the suffixes. The former one may be grouped under the exocentric type and the latter one under the endocentric type. We have also analysed various meaning - *adhikāra*-s that are noticed in TF.

The following chapter gives a Conclusion and Remarks of the present work.

REFERENCES

1. *English Word-Formation*, p. 140.
2. For details see Lyons, J., *Introduction to Theoretical Linguistics*, pp. 470-80; *Semantics* Vol. I, pp. 286-87.
3. Aronoff, M., *Word-Formation in Generative Grammar*, p. 50; Lyons, J., *Semantics* Vol. II, pp. 409-22; Scalise, *Generative Morphology*, p. 53.
4. This rule may be treated as a regular WFR.
5. *Semantics*, Vol. II, p. 542.
6. *The Morphological and Semantics Regularities in the Lexicon*, p. 655.
7. For details on Pragmatics See Lyons, J., *Semantics*, Vol.I, pp. 114-119; Clark and Clark, *When Nouns as Surface Verbs*; Bauer, L., *English Word-Formation*, p. 85.
8. Subrahmanyam, P.S., *Deep Structure and Surface Structure in Pāṇini*, pp. 346-66.
9. See Joshi, S.D., *Samarthāhnika*; Murthi, M.S., *Sanskrit Compounds: A Philosophical Study*; Deshpande, M.M., *Evolution of Syntactic Theory in Sanskrit Grammar: Syntax of the Sanskrit Infinitive - tunUN*; Mahavir, *Samartha Theory of Panini*.
10. Pāṇini's *Taddhita-Affixation Rules*, p. 11.
11. Subrahmanyam, P.S., *Panini's Use of Semantics*, p. 132.
12. *Ṭābṛci* (A.4.1.9).
13. Lyons, J., *Introduction to Theoretical Linguistics*.
14. See Sec. 5.4. in the present work.
15. *anirdhārita viśeṣerthe yadā prakṛtirvartate, tadā tad viśeṣadyotanāya svārthikaḥ pratyayaḥ vidhīyate*/Kaiyata on A.5.3.74.
16. *prakṛtyartha viśeṣaṇaṃ ca svārthikānām dyotyam bhavati/Kāsika*, A.5.3.53.
17. Under the rule A.5.4.7 Patañjali enumerates the obligatory suffixes such as *tamaPādyaḥ prākkanaḥ* etc.

18. *Kāśikā*, A.4.1.82.
19. A.5.4.29.
20. *Linguistic Analysis and Some Indian Traditions*, pp. 42-43.
21. *atyanta svārthikānām subutpatteḥ pūrvameva pravṛttiḥ* - *Udyota*, A.4.1.48.
22. A.4.1.82.
23. See Sec. 1.0.5. in the present work.
24. Bhate, S., *The Meaning-Adhikāra*-s *in the Taddhita-section of the Aṣṭādhyāyī*, p. 81.
25. *Ibid.*, p. 82.
26. See Sec. 5.3.1.2. in the present work.
27. See Sec. 3.1.1.2. in the present work.
28. *MBh* on *A.* 5.2.94.

CHAPTER - VI

CONCLUSION AND REMARKS

6.0. In the Pāṇinian tradition we notice two types of stems and roots, namely, (1) simple and (2) complex which are underived and derived respectively. The underived nominal stem is technically termed *prātipadika* — a meaningful element; and, it is different from other meaningful elements such as a verbal root, suffix and the like. Further, the verbal roots that are underived are enjoined in the aphorism *bhūvādaya dhātvaḥ* (*A*.1.3.1) as the class of expressions whose first number is *bhū*, *vā*, etc. However, all the verbal roots have been exhaustively enumerated by Pāṇini in his work *dhātupāṭha* with their linguistic features.

6.0.1. The second type namely, the complex nominal stem is derived from an existing item either by the addition of suffixes or by the addition of an existing word to it. Such nominal stems are referred to in the aphorism *kṛttaddhitasamāsāśca* (*A*.1.2.46). That is, the meaningful elements which are derived by the addition of *kṛt* and *taddhita*-suffixes and nominal stems which are compounded are also designated as *prātipatika*. Similarly, the second type of verbal roots are also derived from the existing verbal roots as well as the nominal bases by the addition of suffixes such as - *saN* and the like. This type of roots is referred to in the rule *sanādyantā dhātavaḥ* (*A*.3.1.32) which means that 'that is the root which has at its end suffixes such as - *saN* and the like'.

6.0.2. The derived nominal stems and the verbal roots are characterised as *vṛtti*-s[1] which come under the purview of *padavidhi* — Word-Formation. The latter occupies an important place in grammatical description of Sanskrit language. In our investigation we have restricted the scope of this work to the discussion on *Taddhita*-Formation only on the following ground. The process of *Taddhita*-Formation belongs to the secondary type of Word-Formation in the Pāṇinian tradition. It involves the complexity of the meaning and the suffixation on the one hand, and the various phonological rules that operate from inside and outside the domain of TF on the other. For a detailed exposition of such complex phenomena we had taken up for study the *Taddhita*-Formation. This study is modelled upon Aronoff's Theory of Word-Formation.

6.1.1. In the present work, we have studied the process of TF from the stand-point of Modern Linguistics under the following heads: (1) base; (2) suffix; (3) case-ending in the construction/the underlying sentence; (4) some morpho-phonological operation; and (5) semantics.

6.1.2. Of these, the base and the suffix have been dealt with under the Morphological Features of the *Taddhita*-Formation. Generally the base for the TS is a nominal word. Sometimes nominal stems, pronouns, adjectives and adverbs also serve as bases in a restricted manner. In this regard we have discussed elaborately (3.1) on the restriction of suffixes to specific bases based upon different linguistic conditions, namely, phonological, lexical and semantics. Among these, the lexical condition plays a vital role in TF. By this process all the TS-s have been classified into six major groups. And, each group consists of a general suffix such as -*aṆ* and the like, along with the regular exceptions conditioned by the linguistic factors noticed above.

6.2. Moreover, case-ending (word) in a sentence that is, in the US is often times used in TF. The case-ending that is specified in a US provides us with both syntactic and semantic relations of the output. It is because, the *asvārthika*-types of suffixes are added to the first member of the US in a given context. In the process of TF the case-ending of the base is dropped, and thus from the output or the surface level one could not comprehend the intended sense. It can be known only from the US or the source from which the output is derived. From this point of view the TF is classified into Syntactic and Lexical Derivation. The former one is derived from a US and the latter is just derived by the addition of a suffix to the base that is specified in the TFR-s. Further, the *Taddhita*-derivatives which are derived from a US express the *Kāraka* and the non-*kāraka* relation through their underlying case-endings. Thus we notice all the seven case-ending words which have been employed to prescribe the TS-s. We have also discussed with the notion of productivity as it is applied to morphological process. Thus the Syntactic Derivation is more productive than the Lexical one in view of the fact that the TS-s which belong to the former type are enjoined in such a manner that they can be applied to any kind of bases other than the exceptional ones. In the latter case the base, and the suffix are specified accordingly. Though the TS-s are large in number, yet they can be simplified by adopting the above method of classification.

6.3.1. As far as the morpho-phonological operations are concerned, Pāṇini's rules that prescribe the morpho-phonological changes are not always found arranged according to their successive application; and they are to be known from other sections of the *Aṣṭādhyāyī* and are to be applied in the process of the derivation of the new word. In this connection we notice two types of phonological operative rules, namely, the rules that are enjoined within the sphere of TF; and those outside the latter. The former set of rules enjoins the morpho-phonological operation only in regard to the TF, while the latter one is enjoined in such a way that these rules are the exceptions to the general morpho-phonological operative rules which are applicable for TF. Thus the former set of rules is characterised as TFR-s, while the latter, as AR-s. Such a kind of classification helps us to identify the role and the range of application of TFR-s and the AR-s. Thus the (morpho)phonological operative rules which fall within the domain of *Taddhita*-section may be characterised as Internal Phonological Operative Rules, while the rules that fall outside the domain of *Taddhita*-section as External Phonological Operative Rules. The IPOR-s not only differ from the EPOR-s but also within themselves. That is, the IPOR is different from the other TFR-s that enjoin the suffix or the base or the meanings. The IPOR enjoins some (morpho)phonological operations such as alternation, augmentation, deletion and the like along with the prescription of the suffixes and meanings. On the other hand, the EPOR-s enjoin only the phonological operation and not any suffix or meaning. In this respect the IPOR is different from the EPOR.

6.3.2. The separation between the TFR and AR-s not only makes the TFR simple, but also simplifies the formulation of the morpho-phonological operation in regard to TF. It may be added here that the AR-s generally operate on the output, whereas the IPOR-s are applied to both the input and the output. As we have seen in Chapter Two, the IPOR causes the changes in the meaning of the output, while AR-s do not change any meaning-part of the output.

6.3.3. Moreover, the separation of the (morpho) - phonological operative rules within the TFR-s facilitates the identification of the exact nature of TFR-s emphasizing the productivity of the TFR-s. To be more explicit: the IPOR operates in regard to specific cases only. However, the other types of TFR-s can be applied to any kind of bases. For example, the suffix - *ṭhaK* is deleted by the rule *lavaṇālluk* (*A*.4.4.24) could be applied only to the specified base, that is *lavaṇa*. Thus this is the less productive than the other TFR-s. But the rules such as *prāgdīvyato'Ṇ* (*A*.4.1.83), etc; which enjoin the suffixes such as - *aṆ* etc., are productive ones in the sense that they could be applied to any type of base.

6.4.1. In so far as semantics of the TF is concerned it plays a vital role. Semantic congruence with other words in a US is a necessary pre-condition for TF. That is, a TS can be added to a base only when it is semantically compatible with the other words in the given US. For example, *Vyākaraṇam adhīte* -

vaiyākaraṇaḥ. Herein the base, namely, *vyākaraṇa* is semantically related with the other word of the US, namely, *adhīte* which is replaced by the suffix - *aṆ*.

6.4.2. The TS-s have been classified on the basis of semantic criteria into two, namely *asvārthika* and *svārthika* (See Sec. 5.3). Pāṇini has not classified the TS-s on these lines; but his commentators[2] have divided them into three different groups according to the meanings denoted by them. The former set of suffixes belongs to the exocentric type of constructions, while the latter one to the endocentric type. The *asvārthika* types of suffixes are more productive than *svārthika* types. It is because, the former could be applied to any number of words, while the latter to specified bases only.

6.4.3. There are also some TS-s conditioned by semantic criterion (See Sec. 5.2). Herein some semantic requirements are to be satisfied with regard to the application of *Taddhita*-suffixes. We have discussed the semantic requirements for the base as well as the output in regard to the application of certain TS-s in the section referred to above.

6.4.4. In the Process of TF we come across various meaning - *adhikāra*-s based upon the meaning statements that are stated in this section. Each and every meaning heading governs a number of suffixes. In other words, the same meaning is expressed by a variety of suffixes. In TF, Pāṇini has specified nearly one hundred and seventy five meaning headings each constituting an *adhikāra*. That is, each and every meaning heading is treated as a meaning-*adhikāra*.

6.5.1. Some scholars like Bhate view[3] that Pāṇini has been quite inconsistent with regard to the meaning-types that are stated in TF on the ground that the meaning-*adhikāra*-s which are used in TF are not correlated to the other sections of the *Aṣṭādhyāyī*. Further they argue that he does not follow a single method to explain the meaning-*adhikāra*-s and have come to the conclusion that "the Kaleidoscopic view of the *taddhita* section in *Aṣṭādhyāyī* is due to multiple authorship".[4] The result of their argument is that the TFR-s that fall under the group where there is a diversity in the meaning-*adhikāra*-s are not framed by Pāṇini.

6.5.2. The view set forth in the foregoing paragraph does not seem to be sound. It is because, the rules that deal with the TF are different from the other one's (*kṛt* and *samāsa*). That is, in TF we notice hundreds of the meaning-types, stated in specific context, give rise to many acute complicacies due to the wording of the rules and their arrangement. And this must have attracted the attention of Pāṇini. As very often proclaimed by Patañjali the modes of the TF are variegated and also complicated,[5] hence it is impossible to adopt a single method to explain all the meaning-*adhikāra*-s.

6.5.3. In cases like *svāṅgebhyaḥ prasite* (A.5.2.66) it is argued that Pāṇini has not mentioned the syntactic connection of the stem with the meaning. This, however, does not constitute a defect. For, it seems that the syntactic connection of the stem with the meaning is continued from the previous rule, namely, *tatra kuśalaḥ* (A.5.2.63) by the process of *anuvṛtti*. Hence Pāṇini has not felt the necessity to specify the syntactic connection of the stem with the meaning. In this and similar other aphorisms, the *samartha vibhakti* that is, the *vibhakti* or the case-ending of the first word of the US which is syntactically and semantically connected with the other words of the US is obtained from the preceding rules. In the above instance we bring in the case-ending of the base in the given US from A.5.2.63 where the pronoun *tad* with locative case-ending signifies all the bases ending in locative case in general in the present context. Now where the word *tatra* is provided from A.5.2.63 the rule A.5.2.66 could have been *svāṅgebhyeṣu prasite* according to the method of stating the case-ending of the base or the syntactic connection of the stem with the meaning elsewhere such as *tasyāpatyam* (A.4.1.92), etc. It may be noted here that such observations in regard to the methodology adopted by Pāṇini could not be viewed either as an improvement upon his grammar or as helpful to a clearer understanding of the formulation of his rules.

6.5.4. Moreover Pāṇini is well aware of the convention that the usage of case-suffixes depends upon the choice of the speaker;[7] and this must be the driving force for him to use *Kāraka*-s according to his preference in his own rules. It may be added here that since the *asvārthika*-types of *Taddhita* words are derived from their US, the US-s would normally contain atleast two constituent members in which the first member serves as the base for the derivation (See Sec. 5.4). The words of the US will either be specified within the TFR-s themselves, or will be taken from the previous rules by following the convention of *anuvṛtti*. It comes to this: there is no *asvārthika*-type of *taddhita* words derived without any US; and the US may directly or by convention of *anuvṛtti* could have these words in TF. Thus the unalterable position that a US serves as the source of the *asvārthika*-type of derivation in which the *Taddhita*-section of the *Aṣṭādhyāyī* could be discerned.

6.5.5. Besides, it seems that Pāṇini's grammar has been designed as such taking into consideration various schools of all the Veda-s.[8] Hence it is impossible to account for every formation adopting a single method. Pāṇini's system could be studied from various stand-points. Though he is not the first grammarian of Sanskrit language, yet he is the only grammarian who presented to us the perfect description of both Vedic and Classical Sanskrit including the spoken form of his time.

6.6. From the above study it may be concluded that as in Modern Linguistics in Sanskrit too the Derivational Morphology is a distinct branch of study. Though Pāṇini has treated the theory of Word-Formation as a distinct branch under the domain of *padavidhi*, yet most of the regular WFR-s are syntax-based. That is, the word that are derived by the application of these rules are based upon the underlying syntactic structure. In the place of the derived word the US can be used interchangeably. This shows that the Word-Formation in Sanskrit is dependent on the study of syntax.

6.7. We have, in the preceding chapters, discussed the nature and the scope of Word-Formation in Sanskrit and the various linguistic changes that are reflected in the process of

TF. Further studies similar to the present one may, of course, be taken up. The method of classification of *Taddhita*-suffixes, TFR-s and (morpho)-phonological Operative rules, etc., might be extended to the other types of Word-Formations namely, *kṛt* and *saNādi*. This scheme of description of the other type of Derivational Suffixes would exhibit such kind of Linguistic Features proving that Pāṇini's Derivational Morphology is one of the Descriptively Adequate Systems.

REFERENCES

1. *Kṛttaddhita samāsasa nādyantadhātavah catasro vṛttayah, Mañjūṣā, Vṛttivicāra*-section.
2. Patañjali, Kaiyata, Negeśa and others.
3. Bhate, S., *The Meaning-Adhikāra-s in the Taddhita-section of the Aṣṭādhyāyī*; Joshi, S.D. and Roodbergen, *The Structure of the Aṣṭādhyāyī in Historical Perspective*, Proceedings of the International Seminar on Pāṇini, p. 47.
4. *The Meaning-Adhikāra*-s *in the Taddhita-section of the Aṣṭādhyāyī*, p. 91.
5. *Vicitrāḥ taddhita vṛttayaḥ, MBh.* on *A.*2.4.32 and *A.*6.1.99.
6. Bhate, S., *The Meaning-Adhikāra*-s *in the Taddhita-section of the Aṣṭādhyāyī*, p. 90.
7. *vivakṣātaḥ kārakāṇi bhavanti, MBh.* on *A.*1.4.23.
8. *sarva vedapāriṣadam hīdam śāstram;*
   tatra naikaḥ panthāḥ sakyaḥ āsthātum, MBh.

BIBLIOGRAPHY

PRIMARY SOURCES (SANSKRIT TEXTS)

Aṣṭādhyāyī of Pāṇini, With English Translation by S.C. Vasu, Reprinted (1962), Motilal Banarasi Dass, Delhi.

————, With English Translation by S.M. Katre, Motilal Banarasi Dass, Delhi, 1989.

Kāśikā of Jayāditya-Vāmana, With the Commentaries of Nyāsa of Jinendrabuddhi and Padamañjarī of Haradatta, Tara Printers, New Delhi, 1986.

Paribhāṣenduśekhara of Nāgeśabhaṭṭa, Edited by K.V. Abhyankar, English Translation by Kielhorn, Bhandarkar Oriental Research Institute, Poona, 1960.

Praudhamanoramā of Bhaṭṭojī Dīkṣita, With the commentary sabdaratna by Hardiksita, Chowkamba Sanskrit Prathishtan, Varanasi.

Laghuśabdenduśekhara of Nāgeśabhaṭṭa, Kāśi Sanskrit Series, Varanasi.

Vyākaraṇa Mahābhāṣya of Patañjali, With the Commentaries *Pradīpa* of Kaiyaṭa and *Udyota* of Nāgeśa, Chowkamba Sanskrit Series, Varanasi, 1988.

Vaiyākaraṇa Bhūṣaṇasāra of Kauṇḍa Bhaṭṭa, With the Commentary of Peri Sūryanārāyaṇa Śāstri, Ajanta Art Printers, Guntur, A.P. 1970.

Vaiyākaraṇa Siddhānta Mañjuṣā of Nāgeśa Bhaṭṭa, Saṁpoorṇānanda Sanskrit Viśvavidyālaya, Varanasi.

Vaiyākaraṇa Siddhanta Kaumudī of Bhaṭṭoji Dīkṣita, With the commentaries Bālamaṇoramā of Vāsudevadīkṣita and Tattvabodhinī of Jñāṇendra Sarasvatī, Motilal Banarasi Dass, Delhi.

Vākyapadīya of Bhartrhari Vrttisamuddeśa, With the Commentaries of *Prakāśa* by Helārāja and *Ambākartrī* by Sri Raghunātha Śarmā, Saṁpoorṇānanda Viśvavidyālaya, Varanasi, 1977.

Śabdaśaktiprakāśikā of Jagadīśatarkālankāra, Chowkhamba Sanskrit Series Office, Varanasi, 1934.

SECONDARY SOURCES

(a) *Works relating to Pāṇini and his school*

Books, monographs, thesis, etc.

Abhyankar, K.V. (1961), *A Dictionary of Sanskrit Grammar,* Oriental Institute, Baroda.

Belvalkar, S.R. (1915), *Systems of Sanskrit Grammar,* Bharatiya Vidya Prakasan, Delhi.

Bālasubrahmanyam, M.D. (1981), *The Systems of Kṛt Accentuation in Pāṇini and the Veda,* Kendriya Sanskrit Vidyapeetha, Tirupati.

Benson, W.J. (1990), *Patañjali's remarks on Aṅga,* Oxford University Press, Madras.

Cardona, G. (1976), *Pāṇini: A survey of research,* Motilal Banarasidass, Delhi.

———— (1983), *Linguistic Analysis and Some Indian Traditions,* Bhandarkar Oriental Institute, Poona.

———— (1988), *Pāṇini: His works and its Traditions,* vol. I: Background and Introduction, Motilal Banarsidass, Delhi.

Chatterjee, K.C. (1964), *Technical Terms and Techniques of Sanskrit Grammar,* University of Calcutta, Calcutta.

Chaturvedi, S.P. (1973), *Sārasvata Sandarśana,* Bharati Parishad Prayag, This book is a compilation of Several Research articles of the present scholar, Published also separately elsewhere earlier.

Devasthali, G.V. (1967), *Anubandhas of Pāṇini,* University of Poona, Poona.

Deshpande, M.A. (1980), *Evolution of Syntactic Theory in Sanskrit Grammar : Syntax of the Sanskrit Infinitive-tumUN,* Ann Arbor: Karoma.

Dvivedi, H.P. (1978), *Studies in Pāṇini*, Inter India Publications, Delhi.

Faddegon, B. (1936), *Studies on Pāṇini*, Amsterdam.

Gold Stucker (1965), *Pāṇini: His place in Sanskrit Literature*, Chowkamba Sanskrit Series Office, Varanasi.

Ghosh, B.K. (1937), *Linguistic Introduction to Sanskrit*, Indian Research Institute Publications, Calcutta.

Iyer, V.S. (1972), *Prakriyā Sarvasva: A Critical Study*, University of Kerala, Trivandrum.

Joshi, D.M. (1969), *Paṇini's Taddhita Affixation Rules (Thesis)*, Pensylvania University.

Joshi, S.D. (1968), *Patañjali's Vyākaraṇa Mahābhāṣya-Samarthāhnika* (P.2.1.1), Publications of the Centre of Advanced Study in Sanskrit, University of Poona, Poona.

——— (1974), *Patañjali's Vyākaraṇa Mahābhāṣya-kārakāhnika*, Edited with Translation and Notes in collaboration with J.A.F. Roodbergen, CASS, University of Poona, Poona.

Joshi, S.D. and Bhate, S. (1984), *The Fundamentals of Anuvṛtti*, CASS, University of Poona, Poona.

Kar, D. (1980), *Semantic Basis of Aṣṭādhyāyī* (Thesis), University of Poona.

Katre, S.M. (1968), *Dictionary of Pāṇini*, Deccan College, Poona.

Kiparsky, P. (1980), *Pāṇini as a Variationist*, CASS, University of Poona, Poona.

——— (1982), *Some Theoretical Problems in Pāṇini's Grammar*, Bhandarkar Oriental Research Institute, Poona.

Laddu, S.D. (1974), *Evolution of Sanskrit Language Pāṇini to Patañjali*, University of Poona, Poona.

Mahavir (1978), *Pāṇini as a Grammarian*, Bharatiya Vidya Prakasan, Delhi.

——— (1984), *Samartha Theory of Pāṇini and Sentence Derivations*, Munshiram Manoharlal Publishers, Delhi.

Macdonell, A.A. (1986), *A Vedic Grammar for Students*, Oxford University Press.

Misra, V.N. (1966), *The Descriptive Technique of Pāṇini - An Introduction,* The Hague, Paris-Mouton.

Misra, C.S. (1985), *Śabdānuśasane Utsargāpavāda Śastra Vimarśaḥ,* Kishore Vidya Niketan, Varanasi.

Murthi, M.S. (1974), *Sanskrit Compounds: A Philosophical Study,* Chowkamba Sanskrit Series Office, Varanasi.

Raja, K.K. (1977), *Indian Theories of Meaning,* The Adyar Library and Research Centre, Madras.

Roodbergen, J.A.F (1974), *Patañjali's Vyākaraṇa-Mahābhāṣya-Bahuvrīhidvan-Dvāhnika,* Translated with Notes, Ed. by Joshi, S.D.

Sastri, Charudeva (1970), *Vyākaraṇacandrodaya,* Motilal Banarasidass, Delhi.

Singh, J.D. (1991), *Pāṇini: His Description of Sanskrit - An Analytical Study of the Aṣṭādhyāyī,* Munshiram Manoharlal Publishers Private Ltd., Delhi.

Sharma, D. (1982), *Structure and Meaning,* Nag Publishers, Delhi.

Sharma, Lakshmidhara, S. (1993), A special Study of Taddhita Suffixes of Pāṇini, Unpublished Ph.D Thesis, Rashtriya Sanskrit Vidyapitha, Tirupati.

Speijer (1973), *Sanskrit Syntax,* Reprinted, Motilal Banarasidass, Delhi.

Staal, J.F. (1967), *Word Order in Sanskrit and Universal Grammar,* Foundations of Languages, Supplementary Series, Vol. 5, Holland.

———— (1972), *A Reader on the Sanskrit Grammarians,* Motilal Banarasidass, Delhi.

———— (1988), *Universals Studies in Indian Logic and Linguistics,* The University of Chicago Press, Chicago.

Taraporewala, I.J.S. (1967), *Sanskrit Syntax,* Munshiram Manoharlal Publishers Private Ltd., Delhi.

Tripathi, K.R. (1991), *Arrangement of Rules in Pāṇini's Aṣṭādhyāyī.*

Tripathi, B. (1967), *Taddhitāntaḥ Kecana Śabdāḥ,* Sanskrit University, Varanasi.

Articles

Ananthanarayana,
H.S. (1969), The Feminine Formation in Pāṇini's Grammar, *Indian Linguistics (IL)* 30: 1-12.

———— (1970), The Kāraka Theory and Case Grammar, *IL*: 31.

Bahulikara, S. (1973), Concerning the Structure of the Aṣṭādhyāyī, *IL*, 34.2.

———— (1974), Maṇḍūkapluti, *Journal of the University of Poona*, Poona.

Basu, D.N. (1983), A Case for the Genitive Case, Proceedings of the International Seminar on *Studies in the Aṣṭādhyāyī of Pāṇini*, Ed. by Joshi, S.D. and Laddu, S.D., CASS, University of Poona, pp. 105-9.

Bronkhorst, J. (1979), The Role of Meanings in Pāṇini's Grammar, *IL*, 40: 146-157.

Bhate, S. (1987), The Meaning-Adhikara-s in the Taddhita Section of the Aṣṭādhyāyī, *Indo-Iranian Journal*, 30: 81-92.

Bhattacharya, G. (1984), Syntax and Word-meaning, *Amṛtadhārā*, Professor R.N. Dandekar Felicitation Volume, Ajanta Publications, Delhi, pp. 37-45.

Cardona, G. (1974), Pāṇini's Kārakas: Agency, Animation and Identity, *Journal of Indian Philosophy*, 2:231-306.

———— (1990), Pāṇinian Studies, *New Horizons of Research in Indology*, Ed by Jha, V.N., Poona.

Deshpande, M.M. (1987), Pāṇinian Syntax and the Changing Notion of Sentence, *R.G. Bhandarkar 150th Birth-anniversary Volume* pp. 55-98, Annals of Bhandarkar Oriental Research Institute, Poona.

Devasthali, G.V. (1974), Vākya-According to Munitraya of Sanskrit Grammar, *Charudeva Sastri Felicitation Volume*, pp. 206-15.

Dvivedi, H.P. (1975), Svārthika-Secondary Suffixes in Sanskrit According to Pāṇini, *IL*, 38.

Ghatage, A.M. (1984), Uktārthānām Aprayogah, *Amṛtadhārā*, Prof R.N. Dandekar Felicitation Volume, Ajanta Publications, Delhi, pp. 141-151.

Hock, H.H. (1991), Possessive Agents in Sanskrit-Studies, *Sanskrit Syntax*, Motilal Banarasidass, Delhi.

Iyer, K.A.S. (1974), Bhartṛhari on Taddhita-Formations involving Comparison, *Charudeva Sastri Felicitation Volume.*

Joshi, S.D. (1974), Pāṇini's Treatment of Kāraka-Relations, *Charudeva Sastri Felicitation Volume*, pp. 258-70.

——— (1980), Proceedings of the Winter Institute on Ancient Indian Theories on Sentence-Meaning, Ed. CASS, Poona.

——— (1984), The Role of Boundaries in The Aṣṭādhyāyī, *Amṛtadhārā,* Prof. R.N. Dandekar Felicitation Volume, Ajanta Publications, Delhi, pp. 181-186.

Joshi, S.D. and Kiparsky, P. (1979), Siddha and Asiddha in Paninian Phonology, *Current Approaches to Phonological Theory*, Indian University Press, Bloomington, IN.

Joshi S.D. and Roodbergen, J.A.F. (1983), The Structure of the Aṣṭādhyāyī in Historical Perspective, *Proceedings of the International Seminar on Panini* : 59-95.

Joshi, S.D. and Bhate, S. (1983), The Role of the Particle CA in the Interpretation of the Aṣṭādhyāyī, *Proceedings of the International Seminar on Panini* : 167-227.

Kiparsky, P. (1991 a) On Pāṇinian Studies: A Reply to Cardona, *Journal of Indian Philosophy*, 19:331-67.

——— (1991 b), Economy and the construction of the Śivasūtras, *Prof. S.D. Joshi Felicitation Volume,* Centre for South and South East Asian Studies, University of Michigan, Ann Arbor, MI.

Kiparsky, P. and Staal, J.F. (1969), Syntactic and Semantic Relation in Pāṇini, *Foundations of Language*, Vol. 5, 83-117.

Mathilal, B.K. (1966), Indian Theorists on the Nature of the Sentence, *Foundations of Languages*, 2 : 377-93.

Meenakshi, K. (1991), The Genitive in Pāṇini and in *EPIC* Sanskrit, *Studies in Syntax*, Motilal Banarasidass, Delhi.

Misra, V.N. (1964), Pāṇini's Grammar as a Mathematical Model, *IL*, 25: 157-78.

Nooten, Von, B.A. (1967), Pāṇini's Replacement Technique, *Language*, Vol. 43, 242-55.

Pandit, M.D. (1963), Zero in Pāṇini *Journal of Maharaja Sayaji Rao University*, Baroda, Vol. 12, No.1.

Pandit, M.D. (1964), A Statistical Picture of Pāṇinian Word-Formation, *Padesa Sastri Sammanagranth*, Baroda.

——— (1973), Formal and Non-Formal in Pāṇini, *Annals of Bhandarkar Oriental Research Institute*, Vol. 54.

Sastri, Gauripathi, T.S. (1974), Quotative Nominals in Sanskrit, *IL*, 35: 1-13.

Singh, J.D. (1974 b), Pāṇini's Theory of Kāraka-s, *IJDL*, Vol. 3, pp. 287-320.

——— (1978), Distribution of Verbal Inflectional Suffixes in Sanskrit, *IL*, 39, pp. 59-69.

——— (1981), Phonological Change in Pāṇini: His Theoretical Assumptions, *IJDL*, Vol. 10, pp. 58-81.

Smith, H. (1992), Brevity in Pāṇini, *Journal of Indian Philosophy*, 20: 133-47.

Scharfe, H. (1982), Secondary Noun Formation in Pāṇini's Grammar: What was the great option? *Proceedings of the International Seminar on Panini*, pp. 53-57.

Staal, J.F. (1965 a), Context-Sensitive Rules in Pāṇini, *Foundations of Language*, 1, 68-72.

——— (1966 a), Room at the top in Sanskrit—Ancient and Modern Description of Nominal Composition, *Indo-Iranian Journal*, 9, pp. 165-98.

——— (1966 b), Pāṇini Tested by Fowler's Automation, *Journal of American Oriental Society*, 85: pp. 44-47.

Subrahmanyam, P.S. (1975), Deep Structure and Surface Structure in Pāṇini, *IL*, 36 : pp. 346-66.

——— (1982), Pāṇini's use of Semantics, *Proceedings of International Seminar on Panini*, pp. 127-36.

Subrahmanyam, P.S. (1990), Pāṇini's Derivation of Case Inflection, *Central Institute of English and Foreign Languages, Bulletin*, Vol. 2 : 2, pp. 64-94.

Thieme, Paul, (1956), Pāṇini and the Pāṇinīyas, *Journal of American Oriental Society*, Vol. 76.

(b) *Works on Modern Linguistics*

Books, Monographs, Thesis, Etc.

Adams, V. (1973), *An Introduction to Modern English Word-Formation*, London: Longman.

Allan, K. (1980), *Linguistic Meaning*, [Vol. I & II] Routledge and Kegan Paul, London and New York.

Aitchison, J. (1987), *Words in the mind: An Introduction to the Mental Lexicon.* Basil Blackwell, Oxford.

Aronoff, M. (1976), *Word-Formation in Generative Grammar*, Linguistic Inquiry (LI) Monograph No. 1, Cambridge MIT Press.

Bauer, L. (1983), *English Word-Formation*, Cambridge University Press, Cambridge.

———— (1988), *Introducing Linguistic Morphology*, Edinburgh University Press, Edinburgh.

Bloomfield, L. (1933), *Language*, Holt, New York.

Botha, R.P. (1968), *The Function of the Lexicon in Transformational Generative Grammar*, Mouton, The Hague.

Bresnan, J. (1982), *The Mental Representation of Grammatical Relations.* Ed. MIT Press, Cambridge.

Burrow, T. (1965), *Sanskrit Language*, Faber and Faner, 3 Queen Square, London.

Chomsky, N. (1957), Syntactic Structures The Hague, Mouton.

———— (1965), *Aspects of the Theory of Syntax*, MI Press, Cambridge.

———— (1972), *Studies on Semantics in Generative Grammar*, Mouton, The Hague.

Chomsky, N and Halle, M., (1968), *The Sound Pattern in English*, Harper and Fow, New York.

Cole, R. (1977), *Current Issues in Linguistic Theory*, Indiana University Press, Bloomington.

Crystal, D. (1985), *A Dictionary of Linguistics and Phonetics*, Basil Blackwell, Oxford.

Fodor, J.D. (1977), *Semantics*, Crowell, New Yrok.

Gruber, G. (1976), *Lexical Structure in Syntax and Semantics.* North Holland, Amsterdam.

Hockett, C.F. (1958), *A Course in Modern Linguistics,* The Macmillian Company, Toronto.

Jackendoff, R. (1972), *Semantic Interpretation in Generative Grammar.* The MIT Press, Cambridge.

Jespersen, O. (1909), *A Modern English Grammar on Histroical Principles,* Part I, Sounds and Spelling, London and Copenhagen, George Allen and Unwin and Ejnar Munksgaard.

——— (1924), The *Philosophy of Grammar,* London: George Allen and Unwin.

Jespersen, O. (1942), *A Modern English Grammar on Historical Principles.* Part VI Morphology and Part VII Syntax. London and Copenhagen: George Allen and Unwin and Ejnar Munksgaard.

Kiparsky, P. (1982), *Lexical Morphology and Phonology,* MIT, Cambridge.

Lakoff, G. (1970), *Irregularity in Syntax,* New York, Holt.

Lapontine, S. (1978), A Theory of Grammatical Agreement, Unpublished doctoral dissertation, University of Massachussetis, Amerst, MA.

Lees, R.B. (1960), *The Grammar of English Nominalization.* The Hague, Mouton.

Leech, G. (1974), *Semantics,* Penguin, Harmonds Worth.

Levi, J.N. (1978), *The Syntax and Semantics of Complex Nominals,* Academic Press, New York.

Lieber, R. (1980), On the Organization of the Lexicon. Unpublished doctoral dissertation, MIT, Cambridge.

Lyons, J. (1968), Introduction to Theoretical Linguistics, Cambridge.

——— (1977), *Semantics,* 2 Vols. Cambridge University Press, Cambridge.

Marchand, H. (1969), *The Categories and Types of Present Day English word Formation,* Second Edition, C.H. Beck Muchen.

Matthews, P.H. (1972), *Inflectional Morphology: A Theoretical Study Based on Aspects of Latin Verb Conjugation,* Cambridge University Press, Cambridge.

Matthews, P.H. (1974), *Morphology an Introduction to the Theory of Word Structure.* Cambridge University Press, Cambridge.

——— (1990), *Morphology,* Second edition Cambridge University Press, Cambridge.

McMurray, A. (1978), *English Nominalizations and Derivational Morphology:* A Transformational Analysis. Unpublished Ph.D. Thesis, University of Illinois, Urbana-Campaign.

Millar, G.A. (1991), *The Science of Words,* Scientific Americal Library, New York.

Nida, E.A. (1949), *Morphology: The Descriptive Analysis of Words,* The University of Michigan Press (Ann. Arbor)

Nasr, R.T. 91980), *The Essentials of Linguistic Science,* Longman Group Ltd'., Longman House, Burnt Mill Harlow, ESSEX.

Ostler, N.D.M. (1975), Case-Linking. A Theory of Case and Verb Diathesis applied Classical Sanskrit, Ph.D. Thesis, University of Oxford.

Pulman, S.G. (1983), *Word Meaning and Belief,* Croom Helm Ltd., Provident House, Burrel Row, Backenham.

Radford, A. (1981), *Transformational Syntax,* Cambridge University Press, Cambridge.

Robins, R.H. (1964), *General Linguistics: An Introductory Survey.* Longman, London.

Scalise, S. (1986), *Generative Morphology,* Foris Publications, Dodrecht-Holland/Riverton - USA.

Selkirk, E.O. (1983), *The Syntax of Words,* LI Monograph No. 7, MIT Press, Cambridge.

Siegel, D. (1979), *Topics in English Morphology.* Garland, New York.

Whitney, W.D. (1962), *Sanskrit Grammar,* Mothilal Banarasidass, Delhi.

Zimmer, K. (1964), *Affixed Negation in English and other Languages: An Investigation of Restricted Productivity.* Supplementary to Word, Monograph 5. New York.

Articles

Ananthanarayana, H.S. (1988), Sanskrit and Linguistics, *IL* 49, pp. 115-20.

Anderson, S.R. (1982), Where's Morphology, *LI* 13, pp. 571-612.

Aronoff, M. (1983), A Decade of Morphology and Word-Formation. *Annual Review of Anthroplogy,* 12, pp. 355-75.

Baldi, P. (1983), On some Recent Claims in Morphological Theory, *General Linguistics* 23, pp. 171-90.

Beard, R. (1976), A Semantically Based Model of a Generative Lexical Word-Formation Rule for Russian Adjective, *Language* 52, pp. 108-20.

——— (1993), Simultaneous Dual Derivation in Word-Formation, *Language,* 69, pp. 716-741.

Borer, H. (1991), The Causative-Inchoative Alternation: A Case Study in Parallel Morphology, *The Linguistic Review.* 8, pp. 119-58.

Carrier, J. (1979), Review of Aronoff's Word-Formation in Generative Grammar, *Language* 55, pp. 414-23.

Chomsky, N. (1970), Remarks on Nominalization, Jacobs & Rosenbaum Eds. 184-221.

Clark, E. and Clark, H. (1979), When Nouns Sufrace as verbs, *Language* 55, pp. 767-811.

Downing, P. (1977), On the Creation and use of English Compound Nouns, *Language* 53, pp. 810-42.

Fillmore, C. (1968), The Case for Case, *Universals in Linguistic Theory,* Edn. Bach, E., Hams, R.T. pp. 1-90. Holt, New York.

Halle, M. (1972), Phonology in Generative of Word-Formation, *LI,* 18 : 54-72.

——— (1973), Prolegomena to a Theory of Word-Formation, *LI,* 4:3-16.

Harris, J. (1978), Two Theories of Non-Automatic Morphophonological Alternations Evidence from Spanish, *Language,* 54, pp. 41-60.

Hatcher, A.G. (1960), An Introduction to the Analysis of English Noun Compounds, *Word* 16, pp. 356-73.

Hockett, C. (1947), Problems of Morphemic Analysis, *Language* 23, pp. 321-43.

——— (1961), Linguistic Elements and Their Relations, *Language,* 37, pp. 29-53.

Hudson. R.A. (1973). Conjunction-Reduction, *Journal of Linguistics*, 9, pp. 303-05.

———— (1975), The Meaning of Questions, *Language* 51, pp. 1-31.

———— (1976), *Regularities in the Lexicon, Lingua*, 40, pp. 115-30.

———— (1977), The Power of Morphological Rules, *Lingua*, 42, pp. 73-89.

Householder, F. (1972), A Problem in Rule Ordering, *LI* 3, pp. 391-93.

Hust, J.R. (1978), Lexical Redundancy Rules and the Unpassive Construction, *Linguistic Analysis*, 4, pp. 61-89.

Jackendoff, R.S. (1975), Morphological and Semantic Regularities in the Lexicon, *Language*, 51, pp. 639-71.

———— (1976), Toward a Explanatory Semantic Representation, *LI*, 7, pp. 89-150.

———— (1981), On Katz's Autonomous Semantics, *Language*, 57, pp. 425-35.

Kastovsky, D. (1977), Word-Formation, or: At The Cross Roads of Morphology Syntax, Semantics and the Lexicon, *Folia Linguistica*, 10, pp. 1-33.

Katz, J.J. and Fodor, J.A. (1963), The Structure of a Semantic Theory, *Language* 39, pp. 170-210.

Lakoff, G. (1970), Global Rules, *Language*, 46, pp. 627-39.

Langacker, R.W. (1978), The Form and Meaning of The English Auxiliary, *Language* 54, pp. 853-82.

Leontev, A.A. (1965), The Concept of the Formal Grammatical Word, *Linguistics An International Review*, 15, pp. 33-39.

Liber, R. (1982), Allomorphy, *Linguistic Analysis*, 10, pp. 27-52.

———— (1983), Argument Linking and Compounds in English. *LI* 14:2 pp. 251-85.

Lightner, T. (1975), The Role of Derivational Morphology in Generative Grammar, *Language* 51, pp. 617-38.

Longacre, R.E. (1966), Prolegomena to Lexical Structure, *Linguistics: An International Review* 27, pp. 65-91.

McCarthy, J.J. (1981), A Prosodic Theory of Non-Concatenative Morphology, *LI*, 12, pp. 373-418.

McCawley, J.D. (1968 a), Concerning the Base Component of a Transformational Grammar, *Foundations of Language*, 4, pp. 243-69.

Miller, G.A. (1978), Semantic Relations among Words. In M. Halle, J. Bresnan and G.A. Miller (eds.) *Linguistic Theory and Psychological Reality*, MIT Press, Cambridge.

Miller, R.L. (1966), The Word and its Meaning, *Linguistics: An International Review* 28, pp. 90-96.

Newmeyer, F. (1971), The Source of Derived Nominals in English, *Language* 47, pp. 786 96.

Nida, E.A. (1972), The Identification of Morphemes, *Language* 24, pp. 414-441.

Pesetsky, D. (1985), Morphology and Logical From, *LI* 16:2, pp. 193-246.

Roeper, T. and Siegel, M. (1978), A Lexical Transformation for Verbal Compounds, *LI*, 9, pp. 199-260.

Ross, J.R. (1969), Adjectives as Noun Phrases. In Reibel, D. and Schane, S. (eds.) *Modern Studies in English*, Prentice-Hall, New York.

Sadock, J. (1980), Noun Incorporation in Greenlandic, *Language* 56, pp. 300-19.

Singh, R. (1988), Do we really want a Syntax Organ? A Note on Phonology Morphology and the Autonomy Thesis, *Ll*, 49, pp. 109-113.

Smith, L.A. (1982), An Analysis of Affixal Verbal Derivation and Complementation in Labrador Dhuttut, *Linguistic Analysis*, 10, pp. 161-89.

Stanley, R. (1967), Redundancy Rules in Phonology, *Language* 43, pp. 393-437.

Strauss, S. (1979), Against Boundary Distinctions in English Morphology, *Linguistic Analysis*, 5, pp. 387-419.

——— (1980), How Abstract is English Morphology?, *Glossa* 14, pp. 89-112.

Wasow, T. (1976), McCawley on Generative Semantics. Linguistic Analysis, 2: 279-301.

Williams, E. (1980), Predication, *LI* II, pp. 203-38.

——— (1981), On the Notions 'Lexically Related' and 'Head of a Word', *LI* 12, pp. 245-73.

Winter, W. (1964), From and Meaning in Morphological Analysis, *Linguistics: An International Review* 3, pp. 5-18.

Zwicky, A.M. (1958 a), Clitics and Particles, *Language* 61, pp. 283-305.

Zwicky, A.M. (1958 c), Heads, *Journal of Linguistics*, 21, pp. 1-29. Zwick, A.M. and Pullum,

G.K. (1983), Clitization Vs. Inflection English N 'T', *Language* 59, pp. 502-13.

INDEX